PRAISE FOR *BUI* *CULTURAL AGILI*. .

"The world of work has evolved dramatically over the past few decades. In the area of employee development, companies are embracing new models and practices. The new models include a more strategic adoption of pro bono and skills-based volunteerism. For managers to develop, they need to build a variety of competencies that can be gained through strategic volunteerism. Among these essential competencies, cultural agility has become a game-changer. In *Build Your Cultural Agility*, Paula Caligiuri shares her wisdom in a compelling and practical book for all employees and supervisors. This book will become a valuable read for global managers in all industries."
Michael Bzdak, Global Director, Employee Engagement, Johnson & Johnson, author, *Corporate Cultural Responsibility: How Business Can Support Art, Design and Culture*, Graduate Faculty, School of Communication and Information, Rutgers University

"The value of cultural agility is amplified in today's global business economy. In her book, *Build Your Cultural Agility*, Paula Caligiuri leverages her expertise in this space to pose thought provoking questions, offer viable options for development, and share key takeaways to advance and build critical cultural competencies that make an impact. This book is a must for any current or aspiring global professional. The world isn't slowing down, neither should you. If you want to be more effective in intercultural situations, this book is an excellent guide!"
Victoria Di Santo, Director, Organizational Development & Effectiveness, Brother International Corporation

"For those in search of a successful international career, or those looking to support the growth of global talent in their organization, this book is packed with practical advice on how to be effective in cross-cultural situations. What is particularly interesting in this book is the compelling argument that the same practices that help us to be culturally agile in an international setting can also make us more effective in navigating the prevalent subcultures – organizational, professional, generational – that surround us. As a trusted adviser to leading

companies across the globe for more than three decades, I highly recommend Paula's research-backed thinking and advice on how to build cultural agility and a more robust pipeline of global talent."
Michael Elia, CEO, TraQs

"If you want to master handling yourself well in and with different cultures, both quickly and effectively, this book is a must read! Having worked in several countries with many different nationalities, I found this absolutely useful for adapting to various environments. With *Build Your Cultural Agility* Paula has managed to create awareness on the different layers within cultural agility and how to assess one's own position. But more importantly it provides simple instruments to help overcome challenges that can rise through cultural differences. This book has made both my professional and personal life as a globetrotter much, much easier."
Paul Grommel, People Practices, DPR Construction

"The world economy is rapidly becoming multipolar. For managers to succeed in the new era, cultural agility is becoming more critical, by the day. In fact, one does not even have to cross continents to witness the reality of cultural heterogeneity. Just look at the enormous cultural differences within the United States, within Europe, within Asia, as well as within other regions. In *Build Your Cultural Agility*, Paula Caligiuri has written an extremely practical book. It offers managers at all levels crisp tools to assess one's current cultural agility, ideas regarding how to behave, and guidelines for how to further build cultural competence. An essential read for the global manager."
Anil K. Gupta, co-author, *The Quest for Global Dominance*, Michael Dingman Chair in Strategy and Globalization, Smith School of Business, The University of Maryland

"To succeed in today's global economy, people must become adaptable, flexible, and comfortable when encountering other cultures – a concept Paula Caligiuri calls "cultural agility." In this comprehensive and impressive new book, Dr. Caligiuri expertly details the key capabilities necessary for developing cultural agility when working with others, executing professional tasks, making decisions, and building relationships. The book is well-researched and contains useful self-assessments throughout for readers to engage with the content as they read along. An excellent resource for anyone interested in the topic of cultural adjustment and adaptation."
Andy Molinsky, author of *Global Dexterity* and *Reach*, Professor of International Management and Organizational Behavior, Brandeis University

"Understanding cultural differences and developing intercultural skills are necessary for leaders who seek to effectively navigate today's complex world. Professionals and institutions need to become interculturally effective in order to address global challenges such as sustainability while also building the organizational capabilities that allow for innovation and success in local markets. *Build Your Cultural Agility* provides a helpful framework for understanding what these intercultural competencies are, how they work, and how they can be developed. This practical guide helps readers assess and build the intercultural competencies needed to successfully navigate situations of cultural novelty. In addition, the book's structure and pedagogical approach helps readers understand the WHYs and the HOWs by providing real examples and suggested calls to action. Paula Caligiuri's book provides academics and practitioners with an indispensable manual to improving our understanding and mastering of cross-cultural management."
Marta Muñiz Ferrer, CEO, Schiller International University

"The ability to work across cultural boundaries is no longer a nice to have – every entrepreneur, businessperson and global citizen must be able to bridge the gaps between cultures. In *Build Your Cultural Agility* Paula has provided the framework required for all of us to work effectively across any cultural boundaries. *Build Your Cultural Agility* is required reading for all the entrepreneurs in my portfolio."
Andy Palmer, CEO, Tamr, and Founder, Koa Labs

"Having worked in multi-national corporations and done global work, I wish I had read this book earlier. It is a treasure chest of ideas and practical tips for building one's cross-cultural agility. The nine competencies provide a useful roadmap to navigate the challenges of working and leading cross-culturally. Reading about the three task management competencies took me back to my days as a leader making decisions in a cross-country context. Wish I had these heuristics then to guide my decision making – knowing what strategy is more appropriate when. The book is an absolute "must read" for anyone doing global work today."
Pradnya Parasher, Founder & CEO, ThreeFish Consulting and co-author, *The Secret Life of Organizations*

"As a global HR executive, I find Dr. Caligiuri's book to be timely and pertinent. The world is continuing to rapidly evolve, and while doing business across borders has become more commonplace, it has also become more complex. Understanding your own unique cultural lens and adapting your approach to ensure inclusion and respect for others is key to success in any language. The current environment with the global pandemic has only made this book more important. While travel and physical cues used to serve as a key guidepost, providing more immediate feedback for global leaders, we are now faced with a largely virtual environment. Dr Caligiuri's pragmatic guidance on all 9 competencies comprising cultural agility, as well as her focus on developing trust, continuous learning, thoughtful communications and strong relationships are critical for all global leaders to embrace to maximize their impact."

Nicolette Sherman, Chief Human Resources Officer, Oyster Point Pharma, Inc.

"As a global mobility professional and thought leader, I appreciate deeply how Dr. Caligiuri quickly establishes the principles underlying cultural agility and provides a "how to guide" to improve upon or develop foundational elements contributing to cultural adaptiveness. The timeliness of this book cannot be overstated as an effective tool for corporate leaders, HR practitioners, and career-climbers to elevate DEI initiatives through mindful practices and personal accountability. It is no secret that the greatest success comes when we focus on inclusive and diverse teams!"

LaShell Tinder, Executive Board Member, Families in Global Transition

"Cultural agility is a key competency for effective global leaders everywhere today yet it is mostly misunderstood. Cultural agility is much more than awareness. This competency is needed for globally oriented organizational performance and execution as well as for working through the range of strategic options and leveraging diverse talent to chart a truly global business future. Paula Caligiuri's new book takes her academic thought leadership and deep experience in this space into practical, real and tangible action items for leaders thinking and working strategically in the global world of mobility, connectivity and diversity. Thoroughly recommended."

Ian C. Woodward, Professor, INSEAD and co-author, *The Phoenix Encounter Method: Lead Like your Business is on Fire!*

Build Your Cultural Agility

The Nine Competencies of Successful Global Professionals

Paula Caligiuri

KoganPage

Publisher's note
Every possible effort has been made to ensure that the information contained in this book is accurate at the time of going to press, and the publishers and authors cannot accept responsibility for any errors or omissions, however caused. No responsibility for loss or damage occasioned to any person acting, or refraining from action, as a result of the material in this publication can be accepted by the editor, the publisher or the author.

First published in Great Britain and the United States in 2021 by Kogan Page Limited

2nd Floor, 45 Gee Street
London
EC1V 3RS
United Kingdom
www.koganpage.com

122 W 27th St, 10th Floor
New York, NY 10001
USA

4737/23 Ansari Road
Daryaganj
New Delhi 110002
India

Kogan Page books are printed on paper from sustainable forests.

ISBNs
Hardback 978 1 78966 661 8
Paperback 978 1 78966 659 5
Ebook 978 1 78966 660 1

British Library Control Number

2021930556

Library of Congress Cataloging-in-Publication Data

A CIP record for this book is available from the British Library.

Typeset by Hong Kong FIVE Workshop, Hong Kong
Print production managed by Jellyfish
Printed and bound by CPI Group (UK) Ltd, Croydon CR0 4YY

To my Mom, with love and gratitude

CONTENTS

01 Cultural agility for intercultural effectiveness 1
Cross-cultural differences 2
Understanding cross-cultural differences 3
How we learn cultural norms 5
A framework to understand cultural differences 6
What is cultural agility? 15
Cultural agility for intercultural effectiveness 16
The cultural agility competencies 18
Endnotes 19

PART ONE Self-management competencies 21

02 Tolerance of ambiguity for comfort in a novel environment 23
Tolerance of ambiguity 26
Assess your tolerance of ambiguity 27
Behaviors influenced by your tolerance of ambiguity 28
Build your tolerance of ambiguity 31
Case in point: Martin Brandt in Kenya 38
Key takeaways 40
Keep reading 40
Endnotes 40

03 Curiosity to expand your understanding of cultural differences 42
Curiosity 45
Assess your curiosity 46
Your early-life curiosity 47
Types of curiosity 47
The importance of curiosity for cultural agility 50
Fostering curiosity for cultural understanding 51
Build your curiosity 54

Key takeaways 56
Keep reading 56
Endnotes 57

04 Resilience to cope when cultural differences produce challenges 58
Resilience 61
Resilience as a cultural agility competency 62
Assess your resilience 63
Behaviors influenced by your resilience 64
Build your resilience 67
Key takeaways 73
Keep reading 74
Endnotes 74

PART TWO Relationship-management competencies 75

05 Humility to learn from others who are culturally different from you 77
Humility 80
Assess your humility 81
Humility as a cultural agility competency 82
Developing humility 85
Build your cultural humility 88
Key takeaways 90
Keep reading 91
Endnotes 91

06 Relationship building to expand your professional network across cultures 93
Relationship building 96
Assess your relationship building 98
Personality and relationship building 99
Behaviors to foster your relationship building 100
Case in point: a program to foster relationships across cultures 103

Cross-cultural issues affecting your ability to build relationships 105
Develop the ability to build relationships 109
Key takeaways 109
Keep reading 110
Endnotes 110

07 Perspective taking to empathize and understand people from a different culture 112
Perspective taking 115
Assess your perspective taking 116
Benefits of perspective taking 117
Cultural challenges in perspective taking 119
Cultural differences in the expression of perspective taking 122
Build your perspective taking 124
Key takeaways 126
Keep reading 126
Endnotes 127

PART THREE Task-management competencies 129

08 Cultural adaptation to respond as expected in a culturally diverse situation 135
Situations requiring cultural adaptation 138
Skills of cultural adaptation 141
Case in point: adapting behaviors during the Covid-19 global pandemic 147
How to build your cultural adaptation 149
Key takeaways 150
Keep reading 150
Endnotes 151

09 Cultural minimization to uphold a standard in a culturally diverse situation 153
Cultural minimization 153
Socialization 154
Persuasion 158

Motivation 160
Case in point: Shell's global zero work site hazard project 162
How to build your cultural minimization 163
Key takeaways 165
Keep reading 165
Endnotes 166

10 Cultural integration to create new norms for group success in a culturally diverse situation 167
Situations requiring cultural integration 168
Skills needed for cultural integration 170
Cultural integration in global teams 172
How to build cultural integration 178
Key takeaways 179
Keep reading 180
Endnotes 180

11 Using your cultural agility for career success 182
Avoid cultural agility trip wires 182
Develop from cross-cultural experiences 184
Buffer from culture shock 187
Find career fulfillment 189
Continue to build your self-awareness 192
Stay connected 193
Endnotes 193

Index 194

As a reader of *Build Your Cultural Agility*, you might be interested in MyGiide, an app to help build your cultural agility. You can access MyGiide for free assessments of your cross-cultural values and cultural agility competencies. Through MyGiide, you can also purchase cultural coaching sessions, action plans for development, culutre-specific information, and access to webinars.

Scan the QR code to access MyGiide (www.mygiide.com).

Cultural agility for intercultural effectiveness 01

Most people think of culture as *only* something experienced when in another country or when interacting with people from another culture. This is not true. You can experience cultural differences **without ever leaving your hometown.** Here are some examples:

- Did you attend a meeting where many participants were older or younger than you? If so, you might have experienced **generational culture differences.**
- Did you participate in a conference call with colleagues from a different functional area? If so, you might have experienced **professional cultural differences.**
- Did you move to a new neighborhood? If so, you might have experienced **regional cultural differences.**
- Did you start attending a new school or start work with a new employer? If so, you might have experienced **organizational cultural differences.**

As a keynoter, I have given numerous talks about cultural agility and am often asked, what is the strongest cultural influence? My answer is to describe national cultural differences as being analogous to primary colors. Subcultures, such as organizational, regional, professional, and generational cultures, are like recognizable secondary colors and can also be powerful socializing agents affecting values and norms. In the same way countries have socializing agents, a generation's shared historical experiences, pop culture, technological advancement, and the like foster a given generation's culture. Companies also have a shared set of policies, practices, values, and corporate history comprising a company's corporate culture.

This book is designed to help you become culturally agile so you can be interculturally effective in **any** cross-cultural situation—national, organizational, professional, or regional. If you need to identify whether a given group has its own culture and will require your cultural agility skills, ask yourself the following questions:

- Do I feel like I am a "fish out of water" or an outsider when I am with this group (if I am not part of this group)?
- Can I see behaviors and sense that values are shared by many members?
- Are these behaviors and values relatively stable within the group?
- Does the group shape the newcomers' behaviors and values?

Answering "yes" to these questions means you are in a situation requiring cultural agility.

Cross-cultural differences

What comes to mind when you think about cross-cultural differences? If you are like most, you thought of:

- an interesting—or possibly embarrassing—experience you had when traveling to another country,
- a time when you were surprised to try unfamiliar ethnic cuisine and learn that the restaurant's definition of "spicy" was different from your own,
- or maybe a frustration you had working with a colleague who was from a different country.

Whether producing interest, embarrassment, surprise, or frustration, these experiences share the same reality: what you **experienced** was different from what you had **expected.** Our brains are hardwired to interpret—and then expect—certain things based on its [insert your age here] years of stored data. The mismatch between *what you expect to experience* through your brain's perceptual lens and *what you experience* is the definition of a cultural difference. Oversimplifying a bit, the wider the range of different experiences you have stored, the wider your brain's range of possible interpretations for any new situation.

Your expectation for what qualifies as "spicy" is a nice example. If you are not from a culture that uses chili peppers liberally in your cuisine, ordering a "spicy hot" dish in an authentic Thai restaurant may expand your understanding. If you are not accustomed to heavy spices, what you consider "spicy hot" may only be considered "mild" in Thai culture. Conversely, if you are from a "chili pepper culture," go to an authentic Irish pub and order something spicy. I would be willing to bet you did not even detect heat. If either experience was novel to you, then your definition of spicy became wider. If you had already had both experiences, then your spicy meter, already wide, did not change. This is how cultural differences work. The wider our store of knowledge for what to expect, the less surprising a cultural difference will be.

Your brain, a reasonably effective predicting machine in familiar settings, is a faulty predictor in novel ones. In familiar situations, your brain can reliably, efficiently, and fairly accurately perceive people, behaviors, contextual cues, and nonverbals. In familiar situations, this speedy processor between our ears saves us cognitive energy without sacrificing too much accuracy. We do not need to think too hard (or at all) to be correct. However, in culturally new or novel situations, the opposite is true. You will be wrong more times than you will be right. Your hardwired brain can only rely on what it has stored, which means that in a culturally new or novel situation, your split-second initial reaction will misjudge the contextual cues and the intended meaning of a person's behaviors, nonverbals, words—or misjudge the meaning of the word *spicy*.

There is a paradox here. Our highly effective "home court" brain, while useful in familiarity, makes us cognitively lazy when experiencing cultural novelty. Our brains are lulled into believing we do not need to put in much effort to "get it right," when, in fact, we do. Neuroscience mixed with novel experiences and stirred with cross-cultural competencies will produce your reaction to cultural differences. This recipe creates the need for cultural agility, the ability to effectively work in different countries and with people from different cultures. To be culturally agile, we need to get our lazy brains off the proverbial couch and train them.

Think of this book (and the MyGiide.com app) like your trainer, blowing a loud whistle or providing gentle encouragement (whichever you prefer) to help you develop your cultural agility.

Understanding cross-cultural differences

Geert Hofstede has aptly defined *culture* as "the collective programming of the mind which distinguishes the members of one group or category of people from another."[1] Cultural differences are what makes generations, organizations, and nations *feel* different when you are in them but not from them. In the case of national cultures, countries are programmers of the mind because, within their boundaries, each country has its own socializing agents. Native-born or those who immigrated to a specific country at a young age share a common history, legal system, art, literature, media, educational system, political system, economic system, and the like. These nation-level socializing agents produce some similarities among their inhabitants as they learn to live, study, or work within the country's systems. Over time, behavioral norms, attitudes, and values are shaped and a national culture emerges.

National culture is the most widely shared "helicopter view" to understand cultural differences because everyone was born into and socialized into a place. Most of the examples in this book will be in the context of national cultural differences because people tend to feel contextual novelty most intensely when in a different country or when interacting with people from a different culture.

At this point, it is important to note that a conversation about national culture, generational culture, or professional culture is *not* an endorsement of stereotyping. Within any group, there is plenty of variance in behaviors, attitudes, and values so every individual should be treated uniquely. Each individual person has their own socializing agents. Culturally agile people realize that it is just as important to recognize individual differences as it is to understand the norms of the culture.

It is also important to note that in some national cultures, sensing cultural differences will seem easier than in others. Michele Gelfand and her colleagues discovered that some national cultures are "tight" while others are "loose."[2] In *tight cultures*, deviation from the social norms is not tolerated and as a result, its citizens have developed stronger neural pathways for behavioral expectations. People in tight culture countries, such as Japan, Pakistan, and Germany, act in similar ways. If you are in (but not from) a given tight culture country, you will quickly sense cultural differences and the feelings of being an outsider. In *loose culture* countries, such as the United States, Australia, and the Ukraine, there are a variety of subcultures which each have their own cultural norms, resulting in greater variation in the determination of acceptable behavior. Because of this wider variation and acceptance of differences, those in (but not from) a given loose culture country might not sense these cultural differences because they are generally accepted.

How we learn cultural norms

Think about how the various groups in your life have influenced you. Are you able to describe the culture of each group? If not, you are not alone. It is often said that describing one's own culture is like asking a fish in water to describe what it is like to swim in water. The fish might not be able to describe swimming in water but certainly knows the difference when it is on the shore. The best way to learn your own cultural norms and values is to experience contextual novelty. You will be able to sense your own culture more clearly when you are in a different culture and have a point of comparison.

Consider the last time you started a new job or relocated to a new place for work or school. Chances are you learned the ropes of the new place by observing, talking to people, and testing approaches. You might have had coworkers, neighbors, or classmates take you under their wings and teach you how to function in the new place (e.g., what day is garbage collected, where is the best place to buy produce, where to park and not get a ticket). You might have been socialized into mowing your lawn more often, being on time for meetings, calling elders by their titles, etc.

Whatever the novel context, you eventually learned what was expected of you. As your brain learned which behaviors to view as "correct," you might have started shaping your own values to align more closely with the group values. Once socialized into the group, you stopped sticking out as a newcomer and, at some point, were able to guess the newbies because they were the ones acting in a way that did not fit with the context. Conversely, if the new values of this group did not align with your own, you might have left the organization or the neighborhood altogether.

This is how culture is created. You are not born with cultural values. Through a process of iterative and successive experiences with people in groups, you are shaped—and help shape—the culture of those groups to which you belong. When you were young, the greatest cultural difference you experienced might have been families in your neighborhood. As a child, you might have observed these families interacting in ways very different from the way your family interacted. Today, you might reflect on the neighborhood from your youth and see those same families as being more similar in terms of cultural values. This is likely true if you moved out of that neighborhood and experienced a wider range of cultural norms at school, work, and travel.

A framework to understand cultural differences

There are three popular metaphors for describing culture: an iceberg, an ocean, or an onion. Icebergs, oceans, and onions have something in common. On the surface they seem relatively manageable, but beneath the surface, they are far more complex. What you can see can be navigated, but what you cannot see can be more challenging. When you are in a novel situation, you will first see behavioral norms and then, over time, you will sense the culture's values.

Behavioral norms are the first impression you will have of a novel culture because they are the differences you observe when you first step off the plane or walk into a new company. You might observe style of dress, manner of communication, foods, sense of order, art, architecture, homes, and offices. Your brain's perceptual lens compares what you are observing to your stored norms and expectations. If your brain signals "different", you are experiencing some contextual novelty at the behavioral level.

Values, unlike behavioral norms, may not be readily visible. Rather, you will sense and feel them as you spend time in the novel context. For example, you might sense informality when you see colleagues joking with each other or observe little protocol at business dinners. You might sense punctuality when meetings start exactly on time and/or when someone apologizes for being late. These two examples of values (informality and punctuality) affect how behaviors are evaluated. Values form the lens through which subjective judgments are made, such as what is considered fair or unfair, good or bad, beautiful or ugly, respectful or rude, appropriate or inappropriate.

When you are in a new context and your brain starts firing off subjective judgments, you are experiencing contextual novelty at a deeper cultural level. Cultural values are even more deeply embedded in those who are socialized into them and ascribe to them closely. Sometimes they cannot be easily articulated, especially to those who have never been outside their home country.

The relationship between behavioral norms and values is important. If you could time travel to different countries 100 years ago, you would see different behavioral norms everywhere you turn. Seeing the differences, your brain needs to do some cognitive heavy lifting to understand the new place. Today, when you travel to large cosmopolitan cities, you see things that look familiar, and your brain, seeing similarity, registers that it does not need much additional effort to interpret the situation. Your brain stays comfortable and "on the couch," so to speak.

This "lazy brain" problem is a significant trip wire and a natural limit on our intercultural effectiveness. While behavioral norms seem familiar, the values underlying that behavior can be quite different. In these mixed message situations, culturally agility is critical because the reality of the situation is embedded in cultural values that are hidden beneath the behavioral norms. When you are lulled into seeing similarity in a novel context, I want you to think "iceberg, straight ahead."

As we start the cultural agility workout in the chapters ahead, we need a cultural framework, a way to understand the cultural differences we are perceiving. In 2001, I created a model for explaining cultural differences that was based, in part, on the decades of scholarship emerging from cross-cultural psychology, international management, and cultural anthropology and, in part, on the stories that were being conveyed by the many international managers with whom I was working. What emerged from both was *eight dimensions of culture*:

- Formal versus Informal Style
- Egalitarian versus Hierarchical Structures
- Individual versus Group Interests
- Transactional versus Interpersonal Relationships
- Direct versus Indirect Communication
- Fluid versus Controlled Time
- External versus Internal Control
- Balance versus Status Motivation

In the paragraphs that follow, I explain each of these cultural dimensions and provide questions for you to consider that will help you better understand where you fall on each of these dimensions.[3] You can also assess your cultural values on these eight dimensions by visiting MyGiide.com.

Formal versus informal style

In groups with greater formality, individuals will be called by their formal titles, dress more intentionally for the situation, and adhere to protocol and etiquette. They will be more likely to judge those who do not do these things as being ill-mannered, impolite, or rude. If you are entering a formal culture, learn the communication protocol (e.g., whether to shake hands with everyone in the room upon entering the room, whether to use a title when addressing a person, the appropriate way to handle a business card) so as not to be written off as unprofessional—or worse.

Informal cultures follow few social conventions and do not judge each other based on what they wear, how they interact, their adherence to certain manners, and the like. In groups with an informal culture, people are called by their first name. There is more casual dress, casual dining, greater use of expression in speech, conversation on a wide array of subjects, more humor in business settings, and, sometimes, greater self-disclosure because there are fewer social norms regulating polite conversation. In informal cultures, communication protocol is viewed as being unnecessarily stilted.

Do you have more formal or informal values? Ask yourself the following questions. The more you agree with these, the more formal you are. The more you disagree, the more informal you are.

- Do you believe that wearing formal business attire demonstrates respect for one's organization and the people in it?
- Do you prefer to use people's appropriate titles (e.g., Mr. Smith or Professor Suarez), as opposed to calling them by their first names?
- Do you think it is more appropriate to have offices decorated with office-appropriate things, compared to personal (or fun) things?
- Do you think it is important that protocol and etiquette is strictly followed so as to not appear rude?

Egalitarian versus hierarchical structures

Groups differ in the extent to which they embrace a reporting structure and appreciate power and authority in the hands of fewer group members. In hierarchical groups, leaders' authority is not questioned, as leaders are expected to have expertise and provide direction. In hierarchical cultures, asking for suggestions is considered a sign of weakness. In hierarchical cultures, you may observe leaders with status symbols, more specific titles, executive perquisites (e.g., corner office, executive dining rooms, reserved parking spaces).

On the other end of the continuum, groups with a loose structure where power and authority are shared are egalitarian. In these groups, power and authority is not granted by rank; rather, they are earned, and there is a belief that solutions can come from any level in the organization. These groups tend to value shared governance, agency, and members' voices. You are more likely to see business cards without job titles, more personal interactions between supervisors and subordinates, and the like.

Do you have more egalitarian or hierarchical values? Ask yourself the following questions. The more you agree with these, the more hierarchical you are. The more you disagree, the more egalitarian you are.

- Do you believe that people at different levels in the organization have different rights and privileges?
- Do you believe it is important for high-level executives to look and act like senior leaders?
- Do you believe that senior leaders should provide clear direction for their subordinates and not have an expectation that their direction will be questioned?
- Do you believe it is the senior leaders who should make the decisions?

Individual versus group interests

Cultures will vary on the extent to which the group members will place the group's interests above their own interests or their own interests above the group's. In cultures placing high importance on the group's interest, membership in a group provides a strong sense of identity, and members will adhere closely to the norms of the group. Acting in a way that the group did not condone would reflect negatively on the entire group and would cause feelings of shame or guilt. For group-oriented or collectivistic cultures, being a member of a successful team, organization, or unit is highly rewarding. In group-oriented cultures, you may observe team competitions at work, greater use of public transportation, open office or communal office space, and team recognition.

In groups valuing self-interests or in individualistic cultures, members will think about their own self-interests before the interests of the group. While the group might have norms, deviating from those norms would not be cause for consternation or concern because the behavior was a personal choice. Since there is greater differentiation across group members' behaviors in individual-oriented cultures, people can comfortably use more than their "fair share" of a space, money, etc. For example, you may observe large houses for smaller families, families with more cars than drivers, a greater use of individual rewards and merit increases, and more personal offices with, oftentimes, closed doors. People in individual-oriented cultures can easily talk about their own achievements, personal contributions, and success without directly acknowledging the broader group.

Do you have more individualistic or group-oriented values? Ask yourself the following questions. The more you agree with these, the more group-oriented you are. The more you disagree, the more individually-oriented you are.

- Do you believe that people work less efficiently when they work alone, compared to working in teams?
- Do you believe the best work is usually the result of a team's effort?
- Do you believe that group members should not express an opinion contrary to the group's consensus?
- Do you believe you should put the group's interests above your own?

Transactional versus interpersonal relationships

In interpersonally oriented groups, members will build trust through long-standing relationships compared to more transactional groups in which members will build trust through evidence of competence and achievement. With groups valuing interpersonal relationships, members will devote time to developing the relationship and building trust before engaging in business. For this reason, interpersonal societies prefer to work with friends and family members because they are the people who will work hardest for you in the role of vendor, coworker, or subordinate. Given the emphasis on relationships in business, there is a high premium in developing one's personal network over a long period of time.

On the opposite extreme, people in transactional cultures will value the depth of individual competence over the depth of the relationship; hiring friends is viewed more negatively because it is believed that objectivity is sacrificed. In these transactional groups, you will experience a greater amount of work conversations at social events, more legal contracts (fewer agreements over handshakes), and more of an emphasis on what one has accomplished as a marker of professional trust.

Do you have a more transactional or interpersonal orientation? Ask yourself the following questions. The more you agree with these, the more relationship-oriented you are. The more you disagree, the more transactionally oriented you are.

- Do you believe it is important to have a long-term relationship with a person before you transact business with him or her?
- Do you believe it is good to conduct business with family and friends?
- Do you believe business relationships will last throughout your entire career?
- To complete an important project, would you trust in a competent friend who is less of an expert over an unknown person who is more of an expert?

Direct versus indirect communication

The difference between low-context or direct and high-context or indirect communications is the extent to which just words (direct) versus the context of words (indirect) are needed to understand the meaning of a message. Edward T. Hall found that in indirect or high-context groups, you will need to fully understand the subtle nuances (e.g., tone, facial expressions, body language) to accurately interpret the message.[4] This is not needed in low-context, direct communication groups in which whatever is said is meant, with little need for interpretation. In these cultures, you will observe more direct feedback being given and shorter written communications (such as email and text messages).

I have found that the difference between direct and indirect communication cultures can be one of the more challenging when working across cultures. Indirect communicators are interpreting the entire context in which a communiqué is delivered and might be told they are "reading into things too much." Direct communicators, on the other hand, read no meaning beyond the actual words spoken and cannot understand why when one thing is said, something else is done.

When in a more direct culture, be certain to speak declaratively, offer opinions clearly, participate in group conversations without waiting for an invitation to speak, and speak persuasively and not in hypotheticals. When in a more indirect culture, ask questions with humility to better understand the context, observe subtle nuances for patterns in communication, be patient, and pay attention to gestures and tone to gain a deeper understanding.

Do you have more direct or indirect communication style? Ask yourself the following questions. The more you agree with these, the more direct you are. The more you disagree, the more indirect you are.

- Do you believe you should provide direct and honest feedback on a person's poor performance?

- Do you believe that openly challenging a presenter's opinions is appropriate and even appreciated to improve the ideas?
- Do you believe you can disagree with a colleague in a meeting without concern for harming your personal relationship?
- Do you believe that you should offer an honest opinion, when asked, even if it means that someone's feelings may be hurt?

Fluid versus controlled time

In some groups, time is controlled and treated as a commodity. In these controlled-time cultures, you can buy time, waste time, and spend time. Some of the things you will observe in controlled-time cultures are meetings starting on time and adhering to an agenda, prompt public transportation, more clocks in public spaces (which are in working order), and people apologizing for being tardy if even only a few minutes late.

Some groups have a more fluid relationship with time, where there is little value placed on punctuality and deadlines. People, the quality of work, personal priorities, and other aspects of life will intervene regularly to control the flow of time. Deadlines, schedules, and agendas are more general suggestions without expectation of adherence. In fluid-time cultures, people will be late without any intention of being rude, public transportation will not have great precision, and meetings might have start times but not end times.

The difference between fluid- and controlled-time cultures can be a source of frustration. Controlled-time groups, which emphasize punctuality, deadlines, agendas, and strict schedules, often misinterpret fluid-time cultures as being unprofessional, lax, and unprepared. On the other hand, fluid-time cultures often view controlled-time cultures as being overly rigid and lacking focus on issues that should matter more than time, such as relationships and quality.

Do you have a more controlled or fluid sense of time? Ask yourself the following questions. The more you agree with these, the more you have a controlled sense of time. The more you disagree, the more fluid your relationship with time.

- Do you believe that if a person is late for a meeting, then he or she is being disrespectful?
- Do you believe that lateness means that someone is disorganized and unprofessional?

- Do you believe meetings should have both a scheduled start time and end time and adhere to a fixed agenda?
- Do you believe time is like every other commodity which can be wasted, spent, and saved?

External versus internal control

The historical roots of some societies reflect caste or class-bound pasts, where one's status in life was determined by birthright. These cultures believe in fate and that your future is externally controlled and not yours to change. If you do work to change your destiny, the change might not be accepted. In internally controlled cultures, there is a dominant belief that anyone, irrespective of background, education, or physical limitations, can rise to power, achieve their goals, and succeed.

Whether a culture has more of an external or internal sense of control will also affect how they attempt to control the natural, physical, and economic worlds. In internally controlled cultures, there tends to be greater risk-taking, innovation, and entrepreneurship because of the belief that the status quo can be changed. In externally controlled cultures, there is a greater desire for stability, security, and predictability. On this continuum, groups will vary on their comfort in taking charge of their own future, their preferences for rules and regulations, their adherence to traditions, and their comfort with change and uncertainty.

Do you have a more external or internal sense of control? Ask yourself the following questions. The more you agree with these, the more you have an internal sense of control over your destiny. The more you disagree, the more externally controlled you believe your destiny to be.

- Do you believe that people can achieve anything in life provided they put in the hard work and effort?
- Do you believe you can conquer any limitation life has handed you to achieve anything in life?
- Do you believe your status in life is not determined from your birth or your family's status?
- Do you believe that people have control of their destinies?

Balance versus status motivation

You might have heard the difference between groups that "live to work" and those that "work to live." The former groups have status-oriented values and the latter have more balance-oriented values. In groups that value status, members will be motivated for career success even if it encroaches on their personal life. In these cultures, you will see people who answer emails and work on weekends, take fewer, shorter, or no vacations, and prioritize work responsibilities over family and personal activities.

In balance-motivated groups the personal and work spheres of life coexist but great effort is made such that they do not interfere with each other. In balance-oriented cultures, the reward of additional vacation days would be more motivating than a financial bonus. You might observe people from balance-oriented cultures taking vacations of two to four weeks (which seems excessive, if not envied, by those in status-oriented cultures).

A mistake that is often made is to perceive those from balance-oriented cultures as being disinterested in career success. This is untrue. Career success can be just as important to those in balance-oriented cultures as in status-oriented cultures. The difference is that status-oriented cultures appreciate the power, wealth, and recognition of career success whereas balance-oriented cultures appreciate the sense of accomplishment, meaningful purpose, and belonging that comes from success.

Are you motivated more by status or balance? Ask yourself the following questions. The more you agree with these, the more you are motivated by status and achievement. The more you disagree, the more you are motivated to have balance in your life.

- Do you believe it is appropriate that your work responsibilities take precedence over your private home or family life?
- Do you believe it is appropriate to stay in touch with the office while on vacation?
- Do you believe that most people in senior levels of organizations cannot make full use of their vacation time because their professional obligations would make it difficult to be away that long?
- Do you believe it is important to work late to get ahead in your career?

What is cultural agility?

The concept of cultural agility follows what we know about physical agility—the ability to change the position of your body without losing balance. Everyone responds differently when experiencing the cultural differences in situations of contextual novelty. Some are steady while others lose their balance, so to speak. The differences in these responses are a function of the differences in our cultural agility.

Culturally agility is the ability to be comfortable and effective in situations of cultural novelty. As a mix of "nature and nurture," your personality, knowledge, motivation, and experiences all combine in a unique way to create your current level of cultural agility.

The nature of cultural agility

If you enjoy watching professional sports or performance arts, think of your favorite athlete or dancer for a moment. This person likely has some anatomical benefit enabling her or his success: long legs, ideal arm span, petite frame, or higher lung capacity. These benefits are gifts of genetics that facilitated, but certainly did not guarantee, success. Cultural agility works in the same way, as certain personality traits help facilitate your cultural agility.

Personality traits facilitate cultural agility because they help people handle the ambiguity of novel situations and be open to new cultures and people. About 50 percent of personality traits have a heritable component. This means that at least some portions of your personality traits are hardwired into your DNA. As an example, some people are natural novelty seekers. Novelty seeking is linked—at least in part—to the way your body regulates dopamine, a neurotransmitter associated with reward-motivated behavior. You can sense your own level of novelty seeking by (1) how likely you are to try something new, (2) how much you deliberate before making a decision, and (3) how much you enjoy novel situations—or, in the reverse, get bored from familiar ones.

Your genes are only one piece of the cultural agility equation. They are the accelerator—not the engine. In this book, I want you to understand your hardwiring enough to understand your natural gifts (or trip wires) for building cultural agility but be fully confident that you can build your cultural agility from any start point. There is a definite "nurture" side to the cultural agility equation.

The nurture of cultural agility

Think of your favorite prima ballerina or an elite athlete again. Of course, they won some genetic lottery and have natural agility. But even the most flexible dancer or talented athlete needs to learn skills and practice, practice, practice to be successful. The same is true for cultural agility. Cultural agility requires skills and practice, usually in the form of building cultural awareness, social learning, and experience in increasingly more novel situations.

At the most basic level, understanding how a context might differ goes a long way in helping you perceive and understand that cultural difference. A recruiter might explain the unique aspects of your new employer's organizational culture, you might read an article about how to best communicate with someone from an older or younger generation, or you might engage with a cross-cultural trainer to learn about a different national culture before an important business trip. These are all examples of building your understanding of the novel culture before experiencing it.

Just as no one ever becomes a professional athlete by just learning the rules of the game, in cultural agility you need to get out there and put yourself into novel contexts. If this is a new area, your practice might start small by engaging a colleague from another culture and forming a professional relationship. If you are more professionally and culturally seasoned, you might be practicing some of these skills during your next client presentation or global team meeting.

Think of cultural agility more as a practice, not an achievement; and building it is a process, not an event. From wherever you start, the recipe for developing your cultural agility remains the same: gain self-awareness for how you are hardwired to experience cultural differences, and then put yourself actively into increasingly more novel experiences.

Cultural agility for intercultural effectiveness

For centuries, pioneers, traders, immigrants, adventure-seekers, and missionaries have led cross-border lives full of cross-national interactions. They have been driven by the need to relocate, the belief in their mission, or the taste for adventure—propelling them to succeed in their quest, sometimes in the face of seemingly insurmountable challenges for survival. Movies are made from their exciting lives. Their challenges, hardships, and experiences offer exciting tales of triumph and tragedy.

Today, we move around the world with ease for vacations, work, and school. Our passport stamps and personal journeys are not as worthy of movie plot lines compared to the more famous international adventure-seekers of the past. Perhaps they should be. While usually less physically demanding than the plight of Indiana Jones, professionals who work in different cultures face some of the most cognitively, psychologically, and emotionally difficult challenges existing in business today—often without the guide of a corporate compass (policies, procedures, and precedent). They must rely on their personality, skills, and, oftentimes, the assistance of strangers. In other words, they need to rely on their **cultural agility**.

Innovations in technology and communications have created a new cross-national comfort zone for business professionals by lowering some of the initial hurdles for doing business in today's global economy. However, as many seasoned global professionals have learned (often the hard way), mastering time zones and translations are only small pieces of a much larger and more complicated puzzle. Those who can effectively navigate the complexity of the global economy succeed, while those who cannot derail, often taking their firm's business and reputation down with them.

We need more people with cultural agility, but it is a skill that is woefully lacking in the world today. The need for more culturally agile professionals is high. In one large-scale global study by DDI and the Conference Board, 13,000 professionals from forty-eight countries in thirty-two industries were asked to self-rate their effectiveness on twelve managerial tasks; the three tasks with the lowest ratings were the only three on the list with an intercultural component (i.e., integrating oneself into foreign environments, intercultural communication, and leading across countries and cultures).[5] Similarly, the Economist Intelligence Unit surveyed business leaders from sixty-eight countries and found that 90 percent of them reported that "cross-cultural management" is their top challenge when working across borders.

Even in university systems, rich with national diversity, there is evidence of limited cultural agility. According to a large-scale survey conducted by the National Association of Colleges and Employers, only 20.7 percent of employers rate new graduates as proficient in "global and multicultural fluency," while, by comparison, they rate 77 percent of new graduates as proficient in "teamwork and collaboration."[6]

My hope is that this book, in some small way, closes the gap. I want more people to have the ability to comfortably and effectively work in different cultural contexts. The content for this book is based on my extensive academic research in the areas of expatriation, strategic international human resources, global leadership development, and cultural agility. It is also based on my consulting and coaching work around developing cultural agility. I appreciate the opportunity to share what I have learned with you and hope this book helps you in your own journey to develop your cultural agility.

The cultural agility competencies

Cultural agility is a mega competency composed of nine cross-cultural competencies. These competencies collectively enable culturally agile people to be effective in intercultural situations in three important ways, each one corresponding to a separate part of this book.

Part One covers how you can build your *self-management competencies*: tolerance of ambiguity, curiosity, and resilience. These three competencies enable culturally agile individuals to effectively manage their reactions, emotions, and cognitions when in a novel situation. Part Two covers how to build your *relationship-management competencies*: humility, relationship building, and perspective taking. These competencies give culturally agile people the ability to connect with others from different cultures, to communicate appropriately, build trust, and gain the necessary credibility to work effectively in cross-cultural jobs, tasks, and roles. Part Three covers how to build your *task-management competencies*: cultural adaptation, cultural minimization, and cultural integration. These competencies enable culturally agile professionals to make appropriate decisions by accurately reading and responding in the cultural context, while accounting for the business strategy, the key elements of the culture, and the interconnected system of the context, which includes laws, regulations, level of education, and similar factors.

The balance of this book covers the nine competencies that compose cultural agility:

Part One: Self-management competencies

- Tolerance of ambiguity (Chapter 2)
- Curiosity (Chapter 3)
- Resilience (Chapter 4)

Part Two: Relationship-management competencies

- Humility (Chapter 5)
- Relationship building (Chapter 6)
- Perspective taking (Chapter 7)

Part Three: Task-management competencies

- Cultural adaptation (Chapter 8)
- Cultural minimization (Chapter 9)
- Cultural integration (Chapter 10)

Each of these cross-cultural competencies has a dedicated chapter. In each chapter, I cover the importance of the given competency, how to develop the competency with tips for behavioral change, and case examples for the competency in action.

Thank you for allowing me to join you on your journey as you build your cultural agility.

Endnotes

1 Hofstede, G. 1991. *Cultures and Organizations: Software of the Mind.* London: McGraw-Hill.

2 Gelfand, M. J., Raver, J. L., Nishii, L., Leslie, L. M., Lun, J., Lim, B. C., Duan, L., et al. 2011. "Differences between Tight and Loose Cultures: A 33-Nation Study." *Science* 332: 1100–1104.

3 If you are interested in an in-depth assessment of these cultural dimensions, please visit TASCAglobal.com.

4 Hall, E. T. 1959. *The Silent Language.* New York: Doubleday.

5 The Conference Board and DDI. 2015. "Ready-Now Leaders: 25 Findings to Meet Tomorrow's Business Challenges." Pittsburgh, PA: DDI.

6 National Association of Colleges and Employers. February 22, 2018. "Employers, Students Differ in Perception of Graduates' 'Career Readiness.'" https://www.naceweb.org/about-us/press/2018/employers-students-differ-in-perception-of-graduates-career-readiness/ (archived at https://perma.cc/38PB-YN3K) [Accessed March 10, 2018].

PART ONE
Self-management competencies

The next time you have the opportunity, observe people who are "outsiders" or new to a context, whether freshmen during the first week of school, new employees at orientation, or people waiting to go through customs at an airport. You will likely perceive a range of emotional states—anxious, bored, relaxed, or happy—about the experience. There is a wide range of responses when people enter a new context for the first time. How they handle their emotional and cognitive responses to be comfortable and effective in their new context is a function of their self-management competencies.

As humans, we have an innate protective mechanism whereby situations of novelty will evoke a stress response. In the context of working in another country, research has found that when professionals working in their home countries were compared to professionals working in host countries, those in host countries experienced physiological changes in their stress hormones, such as increases in prolactin levels and decreases in testosterone levels. For some, these physiological stress responses can last for several years in the new country.[1]

Culturally agile professionals who have *self-management competencies* are better able to buffer the psychological discomfort, giving them a greater sense of ease in the new environment. They can readily adjust to the new context. The next three chapters cover how you can build your self-management competencies: tolerance of ambiguity, curiosity, and resilience.

Tolerance of ambiguity, discussed in Chapter 2, covers how we all have an internal meter to suppress negative emotional responses as a function of perceived uncertainty. When you build your tolerance of ambiguity, you will be more comfortable in settings where full clarity is not present or possible and, in turn, feel less anxiety or stress in cross-cultural situations. Chapter 3 describes how your curiosity can buffer the negative effects of novelty by reducing the uncertainty in the cross-cultural environment. Building your curiosity, you will increase your knowledge of the new context and, therefore, make it less perceptually novel. Understanding that more mistakes are likely to occur in a novel environment, Chapter 4 discusses your resilience, or ability to bounce back in the face of setbacks. Building your resilience will help you reevaluate mistakes and missteps that can occur while in a cross-cultural situation.

These three competencies are portable and helpful throughout your career. As a culturally agile professional, these three competencies will enable you to effectively manage your reactions, emotions, and cognitions in any cross-cultural situation.

Endnotes

1 Anderzen, I., and Arnetz, B. B. 1999. "Psychophysiological Reactions to International Adjustment." *Psychotherapy and Psychosomatics* 68, no. 2: 67–75.

Tolerance of ambiguity for comfort in a novel environment

02

"You will find treasures—but you need to slow down to see past the rough edges and disorder," said Cheryl Somoano, a global product development and sourcing expert. After spending twenty years visiting vendors in developing countries, Cheryl has sourced everything from textiles to teak for Pottery Barn, a division of Williams-Sonoma. She is now at Palecek, where she both designs and sources the right vendors to create her designs.

As a seasoned global leader, Cheryl listens, asks questions, and observes with a different cultural lens before drawing a conclusion. These skills are critical when sourcing in developing countries. She shared that "things are rarely as they seem when you apply your own cultural lens to the situation in a developing country."

Cheryl gave an excellent example of this. She shared how the female artisans and support staff at factories in Indonesia and the Philippines would rarely speak in meetings—and tended to be written off as not having insights by many of her American counterparts. Cheryl knew that these women, who were closest to their products, had important opinions and that their unwillingness to speak was merely a sign of respect in their culture. Cheryl took the time to invest in trusting relationships with the host national women, an investment of time that paid off tremendously. Cheryl added, "Some of the best-selling product designs emerged from an active collaboration with the host national women who were often ignored."

It is fortunate for Cheryl's organizations that she can handle a higher level of uncertainty for a longer period than most. Without a rush to closure or judgment, she learned that most of her new Indian vendors needed an invitation to provide constructive design feedback, whereas American suppliers are very direct with their suggestions. She realized this when she sent rough sketches to a vendor and the computer-aided designs (CADs) they returned were accurate but not entirely ideal from a product perspective. After some dialogue, it became apparent that many Indian vendors do not like to say no for fear of coming across as offensive or confrontational. As a result of this insight, she knew not to get frustrated with poor-quality CADs and instead made a conscious effort with each vendor to invite suggestions and make it known that their product was a collaboration. Not only did this result in faster sample development and approvals, but her vendors gained a sense of investment in the product and its outcome. This cooperation led to a rapid expansion of innovative products for Palecek within eighteen months of entering the region and yielded some of their most successful designs.

What enabled Cheryl to dig deeper than others in that situation? Cheryl has a natural tolerance of ambiguity. This means that she can feel comfortable—and even thrive—in settings where the outcome is not predictable or in situations that need more time to be fully understood. Like all culturally agile leaders, she knows that uncertainty is part of the job and that any attempt to rush to judgment generally results in a costly mistake.

When she was working in Indonesia sourcing teak furniture, she was venturing into remote villages four hours away by train, sometimes accompanied only by a factory representative who spoke little to no English, with all signs and transit announcements in the local language. In these remote areas, she often needed to rely on hand signals and the kindness of strangers to navigate her surroundings. Even the use of public restrooms was a learning experience that took patience and an understanding of local customs and cultural practices.

Would you find these ambiguous and unknown situations stressful or fulfilling? Many would find them stressful. Not Cheryl. She embraced the novelty and excitement of being exposed to new cultures, foods, world views, and foreign languages. Every country afforded the opportunity to learn about a different way of living.

There is a genetic component to tolerance of ambiguity and Cheryl is proof. She was raised to be comfortable with uncertainty, her parents taking her on backpacking trips well off the beaten path, taking her to the remote

Sierras for snow camping at five years of age, and giving her a "bear whistle" at ten for their forays into unfamiliar wilderness. Both her parents are adventure seekers, having climbed mountains in Africa and kayaked in Thailand.

People like Cheryl, who are wired with an adventure gene, are drawn to the excitement of international work and are often attracted to international majors and study abroad early in their educational experience. In Cheryl's case, by age nineteen she was studying in Bordeaux, France, where she lived with a French host family, took classes in French, and even had a French boyfriend. (It is interesting to note that those wired in this way will also be more likely to have partners who are from another country. In Cheryl's case, she had a long-term relationship with a Scot and lived in Scotland for a few years.)

Being willing to experience more from their international opportunities, people with a high tolerance of ambiguity are more readily able to build their repertoire of cultural knowledge. This experience and knowledge were critical for Cheryl when she was trying to onboard a new vendor for Palecek who made highly unique porcelain décor in the Philippines. In this situation, her colleagues assumed that the prospective vendor's slow response time and lack of communication meant that they were not interested or equipped to take on a new customer. They suggested many times to abandon the effort. But she knew from working in the country previously that Filipinos tend to operate at a more relaxed pace and often lacked streamlined processes for communication and follow-through. It can take an inordinate amount of patience to see forward motion with Filipino partners, but the result is usually worth it. Her wider repertoire of cultural knowledge was critical for Cheryl as she not only managed to successfully onboard the vendor, but the resulting porcelain product became the company's best-selling accessory line immediately upon launch and gave Palecek a firm footing in the decorative accessory arena. A big win thanks to Cheryl's cultural agility!

Cheryl's international career has been vast and varied; she has traveled to a host of countries from El Salvador to Vietnam to find unique products and develop new vendors. Having traveled to Southeast Asia ten times in the last two years alone, she is currently working to expand her company's manufacturing scope into new territories that will bring expertise and innovation to their lighting and accessory categories. For many of her colleagues who are unfamiliar with these territories, Cheryl is relied upon to navigate their path forward with new vendor partners. When she gets on a plane or a

Zoom call to meet a vendor or her sourcing team in another country, she brings with her a critical resource for a culturally agile professional—her tolerance of ambiguity.

Tolerance of ambiguity

Your tolerance of ambiguity is a dispositional trait affecting how comfortable you are in unpredictable, uncertain, or ambiguous situations. If you have a high tolerance of ambiguity, you find unpredictable situations to be fulfilling and engaging—whether stimulating puzzles to be solved or new opportunities to experience. You can be relaxed and comfortable while you learn more about the novel situation you are in. You are, like Cheryl, someone who can be comfortable in cross-cultural situations which hold uncertainties and things one cannot predict. If you have a low tolerance of ambiguity, you will find the same unpredictable situations frustrating, stressful, or anxiety-producing.

The greatest source of ambiguity in cross-cultural settings is an uncertainty about the unspoken assumptions being made—the things that you as an outsider cannot see—and produce behaviors you cannot easily predict or fully understand. These assumptions, rooted in cultural values, are socialized, shared, and reinforced, producing our understanding of what is good or bad, right or wrong, beautiful or ugly, appropriate or inappropriate, and the like. Cultural "insiders"—people from the same culture—do not intentionally hide their values from "outsiders"—those from different cultures. They are just too embedded in their own culture to step outside and explain them.

In a meta-analytic study (a study which merges the results of multiple studies to draw conclusions), Michael Frone found that people who have a higher tolerance of ambiguity are less likely to experience the negative effects of job-related stress that has been caused by working in a context with greater uncertainty.[1] These uncertainties can be major, such as not being able to predict the reactions of those with whom you are negotiating, or minor, such as having colleagues who are speaking in a language that you do not understand. Professionals with a higher tolerance of ambiguity do not experience stress in these situations.

It is also the case that those with a lower tolerance of ambiguity, to make sense of the cross-cultural situation, will be more likely to use stereotypes to explain the situation and reduce the uncertainty. In a cross-cultural context, those with a higher tolerance of ambiguity are less likely to use negative stereotypes because they have no urgency to rush to explain a situation. When working in another cultural context, the ability to withhold stereotypical judgments and take your time to get to know people is important for culturally agile professionals.

In a research study, my colleague Ibraiz Tarique and I looked at the relationship between cultural agility competencies and professional success in global roles, such as managing employees from different cultures or managing a budget globally. Professionals with a higher tolerance of ambiguity are rated as better global professionals, whether working in a different country or with people from different cultures.[2] Even in the case of immigrating under difficult circumstances, tolerance of ambiguity was a positive predictor of coping and well-being.[3]

Assess your tolerance of ambiguity

There was pioneering research in the 1960s on the behaviors of people who are tolerant—and intolerant—of ambiguity.[4] Based on this research and decades of research since, we understand the behavioral patterns of people with high and low tolerance of ambiguity. Adapted from the Frenkel-Brunswick Budner original scale items, the following will help you determine whether you are higher or lower in tolerance of ambiguity.[5]

Read each of the following seven sentences and make an X next to each sentence with which you are in strong agreement. Try not to overthink any question. Usually your first answer is your best one.

- ☐ I would like the excitement of living in another country for a year or more.
- ☐ I believe every problem has a solution. There is no such thing as a problem that cannot be solved.
- ☐ I do not like to plan my days. People who live by a daily schedule miss out on the joy of life.
- ☐ I like mental challenges. It is more fun to attempt to solve a difficult (or possibly unsolvable) problem than it is to solve an easy and solvable one.
- ☐ I have found that conventional and traditional people are generally not interesting. The most interesting people tend to be unique and original.
- ☐ I believe most things are complex. People who expect clear "yes" or "no" answers do not appreciate how complicated most things are.

☒ I am willing to take a leap of faith on life's most important decisions. Most of these decisions need to be made based on insufficient information.

I realize these questions might have been difficult for you to answer because they lacked context. This self-assessment, based on Budner's original scale, is merely a way to provide you with some insight about your own tolerance of ambiguity.

Count the number of Xs you marked. If you have two or fewer checked, your tolerance of ambiguity is likely low. If you had five or more checked, your tolerance of ambiguity is high. And, if you are like most people you had three or four checked, and your tolerance of ambiguity is somewhere in between. In fact, only about 17 percent of the professional adult population has a high tolerance of ambiguity.[6]

Behaviors influenced by your tolerance of ambiguity

Gaining some self-awareness about your level of tolerance of ambiguity is a great first step because this trait will influence behaviors critical for culturally agile professionals, including judgment and decision-making, motivations and interests, and perceptions of trust. Consider your level of tolerance of ambiguity in the context of these four behaviors, using categorization, drawing conclusions, judging others, and approaching novelty. Let's consider each.

How you use categorization

Our brains innately categorize what our eyes enable us to perceive, a process that allows the brain to be activated as part of the fight-or-flight mechanism. It is a mental turn signal, so to speak, enabling us to discern between an aggressive, growling, and unleashed guard dog (run away, avoid, danger) and a bowl of cashews (approach, safe). Categorization like this is functional because it helps reduce the complexity in our lives, as the world around us can be easily interpreted thanks to categorization. We do not need to relearn that an aggressive dog might bite or that cashews are a non-threatening food item (unless you have a nut allergy, of course). This highly functional cognitive sorting through categorization frees up our mental processing power. You can comfortably look out the window to see whether it is too rainy to go for a walk, while eating your nonthreatening cashews. The positive side of categorization is that there is little brain power used in the process.

There is a downside related to categorization for those with a lower tolerance of ambiguity, and it has to do with how we use the categorization to infer attributes about people. Let me explain this concept using myself as an example. As a white, middle-aged woman, no one with the gift of sight, when looking at me, would see a giraffe or an Asian male in his twenties. I am human, not animal; female, not male, etc. To my knowledge, no one has ever mistakenly asked a giraffe to give a keynote on cultural agility. Categorization works as it is supposed to work. When meeting any person for the first time our brains register the visible qualities we observe and categorize the person's sex, race, and likely age. If a conversation ensues, we might start to categorize the person further based on occupation, nationality, religion, education level, marital status, neighborhood, and the like.

The concern with categorizing is not that we see people's demographic features; it is how our brains recall faces—which is helpful. The concern is when one uses those categories to infer the essence of a person, creating stereotypes, racism, and prejudice because behaviors or a category are ascribed to a person.[7] This type of negative categorization is more likely to be present in those with an extremely low level of tolerance of ambiguity and runs counter to developing cultural agility.

But why? For those lower in tolerance of ambiguity, inferring attributes from categories facilitates cognitive order, offering relief for a brain aching from the ambiguity it actively dislikes. A low tolerance of ambiguity greases a brain's slide, so to speak, subconsciously enabling inferences to be made based on categorization. Having a low level of tolerance of ambiguity is more benign when people are working in fully homogenous and predictable situations because one's cognitive categorization system is more refined at detecting subtleties in one's own culture. A lower tolerance of ambiguity, however, quickly becomes detrimental when working in a different country or with people from different cultures because categorization is likely faulty.

How you draw conclusions

Individuals with a lower tolerance of ambiguity tend to draw conclusions relatively quickly to regain a sense of certainty and direction. When people

low ambiguity → jump to conclusions

with lower tolerance of ambiguity are in a cross-cultural situation, their brains innately want to draw a conclusion to move out of a state of ambiguity that the cultural environment produces. The psychological process in play here is like the cognitive process in the previous section; those lower in tolerance of ambiguity are subconsciously drawing conclusions and interpreting what they see quickly to return to comfort.

In a cross-cultural context, fast decisions or conclusions are often incorrect because one's perceptions—the way conclusions are generated—are limited to one's own cultural context. The speedy processor is a flawed one.

There is one more concern of low tolerance of ambiguity as it relates to drawing a fast conclusion: the inability to incorporate new information and revise a decision. Those who are lower in a tolerance of ambiguity, once they experience cognitive closure, do not want to move back to uncertainty in the presence of new information.

How you judge others

Many people with a lower tolerance of ambiguity are prone to black-and-white thinking. Black-and-white thinking means that a person has a difficulty ascribing both good and bad qualities to the same person. Since all imperfect humans have both positive and negative attributes and attitudes concurrently, they are neither all good nor all bad. People who are lower in tolerance of ambiguity seek to make sense of the world quickly and can be prone to using black-and-white thinking as a shorthand to understand another person's behavior.

This tendency is particularly challenging when working in different countries and with people from different cultures because the behavioral triggers for those extreme "good or bad" judgments are culture bound. For example, in some cultures smiling is a sign of warmth, competence, and honesty—traits of someone to be judged as "good." It is a default facial expression when meeting people for the first time in smiling cultures. In other cultures, the opposite is the case. Smiling is reserved for registering true emotion, like joy and amusement, and used only with close friends and family. If a "smiling-with-strangers" person meets a "smiling-with-loved-ones" person for the first time, their impressions of each other might be initially negative. If they both also have lower tolerances of ambiguity and use black-and-white thinking, their judgment of each other will be negative and will remain negative. The complexity and nuances of the cultural differences—let alone the personality differences—will be ignored as their belief in their judgment as correct will stand.

How you approach novelty

Our natural human instinct is to be attracted to the people and things we know as familiar. It is the way we innately judge what is safe and who can be trusted. It is fundamental to how we bond with loving family members as babies and why there is comfort food in every culture. It is natural and human to like and trust who and what is known.

The amazing part about creating familiarity—and preference—is that exposure of even milliseconds in duration can trigger a preference in our minds. The more we experience things, the more we are likely to subconsciously like them. This is true up to the point of boredom from overexposure; even our favorite food or song, while comforting to a point, will be less appealing over time.

From the perspective of cultural agility, the more exposure you have to different cultures, the more positively predisposed you can become to cultures. There is a caveat to this statement. Exposure can increase familiarity and liking *if* your perception of the given culture is inherently positive or, at least, neutral and open-minded. If you hold a negative stereotype about the culture, the mere exposure effect does not work or might even negatively influence your liking for that culture.[8] Maintaining an open mind about a new culture is important for mere exposure to have a positive effect.

Those with a higher tolerance of ambiguity have a natural tendency to seek new experiences, places, people, food, and the like—and have a more positive predisposition toward what they are experiencing. Without actively trying, they feel comfortable with diverse foods, people, places, and the like because they allow themselves to be exposed to those things. Those with a lower tolerance of ambiguity, preferring what is predictable, limit what they allow themselves to experience.

Build your tolerance of ambiguity

Clearly, tolerance of ambiguity is good to have as a culturally agile professional. So, how can you gain more of it?

To answer that question, first think of your present level of tolerance of ambiguity (and each cross-cultural competency for that matter) as having a recipe. Everyone's recipe for tolerance of ambiguity has certain ingredients which combine in different proportions to influence their current, expressed cross-cultural competency. The recipe includes stable personality traits, behaviors, and experiences that mix into the skill one possesses to reduce uncertainty and be comfortable in situations of ambiguity.

The goal is to understand the ingredients and then perfect the recipe that works for you to maximize your tolerance of ambiguity while taking your most natural self into account.

Understand the role of personality in building your tolerance of ambiguity

To understand the recipe for building your tolerance of ambiguity, we need to start with the ingredient which is most difficult to change—your personality. It is important to discuss personality because it acts as a type of accelerator for building cultural agility. Your personality will directly affect your willingness to dive into developmental cross-cultural situations, your openness to new experiences and novel cultural environments, and your willingness to actively engage people from different cultures.

To understand your personality traits, we need to think for a minute about how you are hardwired through your genetic code. Has anyone ever told you that you act just like your mother—or father—or a sibling perhaps? This is a shorthand way for you to see the heritable nature of your personality characteristics. Research has found that about 30 to 50 percent of your personality traits can have a heritable component. This means that at least some portions of your personality traits are hardwired into your DNA.

Tolerance of ambiguity is one of the cross-cultural competencies with a genetic link. As a competency it is influenced, in part, by the gene affecting the system regulating your body's dopamine, a neurotransmitter associated with reward-motivated behavior (among other things). Dopamine is secreted from neurons and attaches to dopamine receptors. The dopamine receptor linked to tolerance of ambiguity is called D4 and the gene responsible for the D4 receptor is called DRD4, nicknamed the "'adventure gene." DRD4 has many variations or polymorphisms—just like eye or hair color. If you happen to have a certain genotype of DRD4, you are more likely to seek new experiences—such as extreme snowboarding or cliff diving—or novel opportunities to work with people from different cultures where the situation is more unpredictable. These more uncertain situations cause you pleasure. You thrive in them. If you had a high score on the self-assessment, you are more likely to try something new and enjoy novel situations—or, in the reverse, get bored from familiar ones.

Your genes, and the role they have on your expressed personality traits, are only one of the ingredients in your level of tolerance of ambiguity. They are the accelerator—not the engine—for building your tolerance of ambiguity, and there are many ways to increase your tolerance of ambiguity.

Practice certain behaviors to build your tolerance of ambiguity

If you have a naturally high tolerance of ambiguity, you are fortunate. Research has connected your high tolerance of ambiguity with many positive outcomes such as happiness, creativity, and a motivation to learn. If your tolerance of ambiguity is somewhat lower, here are some ways to build this important cultural agility competency. You might not want to engage in each of them. Rather, start with one or two and practice them until they become part of your routine or your lifestyle.

Increase your mindfulness

Mindfulness is being fully present in the moment, aware of your thoughts, feelings, and body's sensations. It is important for building your tolerance of ambiguity because those with a higher level of mindfulness are more open to new experiences as they are fully present in experiences without judging them. In a cross-cultural context, mindfulness enables you to take in the new sensations without labeling or judging them through your own cultural lens.

Mindfulness can be learned as it is a skill, a practiced act. Wherever you are right now, sense your thoughts, feelings, and body's sensation. Just be present for a few minutes. If you are eating or drinking something, do so with full intention by actively processing the taste, smell, and texture. As you walk, be fully aware of the sights, sounds, and smells.

Another way to build your mindfulness is through meditation. People who meditate experience a state of mindfulness and learn to be more present in daily life. A place to start is by taking slow, deep breaths. If you are lying down, you can build consciousness for your body, each part separately, from your head to your toes. There are some popular apps, such as Headspace and Calm, to get you started.

Practice reducing black-and-white thinking

Do you use extreme phrases in conversation, such as "That's perfect," "How terrible," "Truly outstanding," or "What a disaster"? My guess is that in your daily life there are few genuine uses for such extreme responses. But, if you are prone to using them, you are engaging in dichotomous thinking, a cognitive pattern which can have a negative effect on your tolerance of ambiguity. These dichotomous thoughts are fostering unrealistic assessments of the situations and pushing you into more black-and-white thinking, the opposite of what you need to foster a tolerance of ambiguity.

Do you know whether you use these extreme words and phrases? If you are not sure, build your self-awareness for black-and-white thinking. Start by reviewing old emails and become aware of your next week of calls and conversations. Make a conscious effort to hear how frequently you use blank-and-white words and phrases. You can also enlist support from a trusted coworker, friend, or partner to flag them for you.

Once you know how much you use these words, you can improve your black-and-white thinking by opting for more accurate—and probably less dramatic—responses. Start to catch yourself and rephrase statements to capture the more subtle and nuanced reality. For example, if a coworker selects a time for a meeting, do not reply "That's perfect"; instead reply "Yes, I'm available." If you are describing the traffic during your commute to work, rephrase "It was a parking lot" to "It took me about five minutes longer this morning." In each example, the former statement is more colorful, but the latter is more accurate. In this context, aim for accuracy.

Your ability to accurately describe, rather than using black-and-white thinking, will serve you well in a cross-cultural context because you are using description rather than judgment. When experiencing a new cultural context, the descriptions will enable you to reflect and inquire about what you are experiencing. You would form judgments only when you fully and accurately understand what you are observing.

Slow your judgment and opinion formation

Do you know how long it takes you to form an opinion or draw a conclusion? In a world where quick decisions and voiced opinions are valued, it is cognitively challenging to delay judgment, withhold opinions, and slow decision-making. If you are like many busy professionals today, cognitive speed is a habit, one which might have benefited you in a domestic context, where you can understand the nuances of the context with some accuracy. Unfortunately, in a cross-cultural context, speed can lead to ineffective decisions and inaccurate judgments. As a culturally agile professional, you will need to slow your judgments, opinion formation, and decisions until you have the time to gather an accurate and complete understanding of the situation you are in.

Slowing your judgments, decisions, and opinion formation is a behavior which requires practice. Here are some steps you can take to build that behavior:

First, recognize your baseline. Over the next few weeks, in your meetings, conversations, and introductions, identify the time it took you to judge a situation, decide on an option, or form an impression about a person. Give yourself "minute markers." After five, ten, fifteen, and every five minutes thereafter pause for one second to rate your judgment—positive, neutral, or negative—about whatever or whomever is requiring a judgment. This is good to do in a meeting where someone is presenting a new idea or in a situation where you are meeting people for the first time. Did your first impression hold in every circumstance and with every person as the basis of your opinion? At what minute marker do your opinions tend to hold?

Now that you know your baseline, try to delay the formation of your opinion actively and consciously. Keep in mind that it is perfectly normal to make initial impressions. Everyone with a functioning brain will form impressions. The problem for cultural agility is not whether you make first impressions; the problem is whether those first impressions hold and affect your judgment and decision-making. After engaging in this exercise, over time, you will become conscious of the speed and naturally increase the time it takes to slow your judgments, opinion formation, and decision-making. Keep in mind that the rate will always be shorter in your home context and longer in a cross-cultural context.

Have experiences to build your tolerance of ambiguity

The previous section offered some suggestions for changing your daily behaviors to increase your tolerance of ambiguity. In addition to the practices you are using regularly, you can further build your tolerance of ambiguity by engaging in some deeper development experiences in other countries or with people from different cultures. Enhancing your tolerance of ambiguity through cross-cultural experiences requires more than passport stamps and frequent flyer miles. (If it were that easy, we could just send all future global professionals on a world tour.) I will repeat this throughout this book: breathing the air of another country does not increase your tolerance of ambiguity—or any other cross-cultural competency for that matter.

The good news is that cosmopolitan business travel has made globe-trotting easier. The bad news is that the homogenization of these international experiences, while universally comfortable, has removed much of the developmental aspects—the contextual novelty—out of the experience.

Large hotel chains, global brands, and the like have limited the contextual novelty you will experience during a typical business trip. Contextual novelty becomes greater when the norms, behaviors, values, beliefs, and communication are different from that to which you are accustomed. For cross-cultural experiences to build your tolerance of ambiguity, you will need to find experiences that provide you with a contextually novel "stretch" opportunity.

Ahsiya Mencin, Brad Jayne, Allison Traylor, and I researched whether international corporate volunteers (employees who were pro bono advisors to nonprofits in developing countries for six months or less) gained cross-cultural competencies from their volunteer experiences.[9] We found that these volunteer experiences did, in fact, build cross-cultural competencies but with some important caveats. International corporate volunteers gained cross-cultural competencies under two conditions: (1) when employees with higher predeparture cross-cultural competencies were volunteering in situations with high contextual novelty and (2) when employees with lower predeparture cross-cultural competencies were volunteering in situations with low contextual novelty. In other words, cross-cultural competencies developed when the employees were given the stretch experience for which they were ready. Too much stretch for some and too little stretch for others did not change their cultural agility competency development. Please read this chapter's "Case in Point" for an example of Martin Brandt, who participated in an international corporate volunteer program offered through his company.

Remember that, for development to occur, the novelty of the situation needs to be a stretch experience for which you are ready. If the cross-cultural experience has too much novelty for you, it will quickly become overwhelming. The heightened anxiety will limit the emotional resources you have for any developmental gain.

Consider the case of students studying in another country. When they become mentally and emotionally depleted from the uncertainty and ambiguity of their host university, they have fewer cognitive resources to engage in developmental activities, such as asking professors for feedback, practicing the host national language, and engaging in personal reflection. These students, feeling depleted of cognitive resources, will seek the ease of being with compatriot students. Being around those who are similar to you will free up some mental and emotional bandwidth. In a study Allison Traylor and I conducted, we found that when students had a lower starting level of cultural agility, they built their cross-cultural competencies when they had a friend who was experiencing the new culture with them and could relieve some of the uncertainty.[10] Students who had at least one close friend with them during the study abroad experience tended to have lower predeparture cross-cultural competencies but experienced the greatest increase in cross-cultural competencies during their time abroad.

The goal is to engage in situations of contextual novelty that will stretch you—but not stretch you so far that you retreat to the psychological comfort of what is known and lose interest in learning about the culture altogether.

One way to think about the stretch experience is to think about the people with whom you will be interacting or the social novelty of the experience. As an example, a business trip in another country where you have little interaction with host nationals is a "low contact" experience from the perspective of social novelty. Working in another country but living in expatriate housing with compatriots from your country and working with people who are socialized to your style of working would be a "moderate contact" cultural experience. Volunteering in a host national community with no one else from your country is considered a "high contact" experience. Ibraiz Tarique and I found that "high contact" intercultural experiences with their high levels of social novelty increased cross-cultural competencies including tolerance of ambiguity.[11]

Engaging with people from different cultures is not necessarily the most natural thing we do, especially for those lower in tolerance of ambiguity. If you are lower in tolerance of ambiguity, you have a natural tendency to seek familiarity to regain the perception of certainty; when given the option to spend time with those from the same culture or those from a different culture, you will naturally gravitate to those who seem familiar. In a study my colleagues and I conducted, we found that for those lower in openness, having structured conversations with people from different cultures produced a greater comfort with interacting with those from other cultures in the future.[12] In other words, if you are lower in tolerance of ambiguity, initial positive interactions with people from different cultures make future judgments more positive. It is a virtuous cycle—when those initial interactions are positive.

Here are suggestions for developmental cross-cultural stretch experiences, arranged from the easiest to the most difficult:

- Invite a colleague from another country to lunch, dinner, coffee, or a drink after work. During your more social conversation, make it a personal goal to identify a few things you both have in common.
- Before your next meeting in a cross-cultural context, whether in a different country or with someone from a different culture, ask a colleague

who knows both cultures—your own and the other—to provide some guidance on how to be more effective in that situation.

- Volunteer in your own hometown, in some situation that puts you in a position of novelty. If you have the gift of sight, volunteer at a school for the visually impaired. If you are young, volunteer at a nursing home. If you have never known hunger, volunteer at a homeless shelter. Rather than volunteering behind the scenes in the kitchen or office, try to volunteer so you are interacting with those who are residents, guests, or clients of the nonprofits.
- Ask to be a part of a global team. Many organizations use cross-border, virtual, and global teams composed of members from geographically dispersed locations. The peer-level team interaction and the common goals can provide rich cross-cultural experiences.
- Accept an international assignment. You can also gain a greater tolerance of ambiguity through living and working in a host country for a year or more. If you want a greater stretch experience, ask to live outside of the expatriate community, participate in immersion language classes, and practice speaking the language with host nationals.
- Accept an international volunteer assignment where you will be working mostly with host nationals. These situations often are the greatest stretch because you will need to adapt and immerse yourself fully to be valuable to the nonprofit organization.

Case in point: Martin Brandt in Kenya

Martin Brandt spent six months in Kenya in 2014 evaluating whether a school program for nutrition and hygiene raised classroom performance.[13] It's important to note that Brandt is not an educator—he's a research scientist who specializes in early drug development for the pharmaceutical giant GlaxoSmithKline. But GSK knows that the best way for its employees to develop global skills is for them to experience cultural disorientation firsthand.

So the company sent Brandt to Kenya to work on a variety of health-related projects. The challenge was immediately apparent. To validate the effectiveness of the program, Brandt needed access to the last four years of data. But because 70 percent of Kenya has no reliable electricity, all records were kept on paper. And that paper was stuffed into shoeboxes and loose files piled on closet floors in one of the rural schools.

No problem. Brandt was ready for obstacles like this, so he set up an appointment and drove twenty miles along rutted roads to meet with the man in charge of the program. "All I was looking for was access to the material," he says. "To me it was a simple request."

Brandt arrived on time—a sign of respect and efficiency in America—but the school leader didn't arrive until an hour later. Okay, different concept of time. Brandt could handle that. "I told him what I wanted and he said, 'Let's talk.' I was there to get data, but he wanted to talk about things that had nothing to do with business," Brandt recalls. "After we chatted for quite a while, I asked him about the files and he said, 'Can you come back next week?'" "When I left I had to ask myself, 'What just happened?'"

Brandt responded by developing a PowerPoint presentation that would show how the data could be used to win funding for similar programs in other schools. When he returned to the village the next week, the presentation went well. The school leader was attentive and seemed interested, but…"He asked me to come back a third time to get the records," says Brandt.

Brandt had two options. He could get exasperated and say to himself, "This is nuts." Or he could adapt.

Because he recognized his exasperation as an American aversion to inefficiency, he was able to control it. Because he was able to see the situation from another cultural perspective, he could see that the man wasn't trying to obstruct the project; he was just doing business the Kenyan way. In his culture, efficiency was far less important than developing a personal bond before work begins. "I had to keep in mind that no matter how simple a solution or a process might be from my perspective, that was not how they did things in their culture," says Brandt. "Eventually business will come up, but it may not be right away. It may not even be that day."

Brandt eventually obtained and analyzed the data. He also improved funding for programs dealing with AIDS and a serious chigger infestation.

When he returned to his job as a research scientist, he had a deeper understanding of how to operate in a cross-cultural setting and greater confidence in his problem-solving skills. But he also said the skills he learned are transferable to the challenges of working within the complex culture of a massive corporation.

Martin, who began the experience in Kenya with a high level of tolerance of ambiguity, ended the experience with an even higher level of this critical cultural agility competency. For Martin, his experience in Kenya was a true stretch experience providing social and technical novelty.

Key takeaways

- Tolerance of ambiguity is critical for cultural agile professionals because it enables them to feel comfortable—and even thrive—in cross-cultural settings where the outcome is not predictable, or in situations that need more time to be fully understood.
- Only about 17 percent of the professional population has a high level of tolerance of ambiguity. This can be increased through self-awareness, behavioral change, and developmental experiences.
- Tolerance of ambiguity has a personality-based component which makes some people feel more naturally at ease in situations of uncertainty.
- Behaviors to increase mindfulness, slow judgment and decision-making, and reduce black-and-white thinking are all important to foster a tolerance of ambiguity.
- Developmental experiences to increase tolerance of ambiguity will get people out of their comfort zone and into progressively more challenging cross-cultural situations. It is important that these situations consider a person's start point to not be overwhelming, inadvertently lowering cultural agility.

Keep reading

- Chodron, P. 2018. *Comfortable with Uncertainty: 108 Teachings on Cultivating Fearlessness and Compassion*. Boulder, CO: Shambhala.
- Fields, J. 2012. *Uncertainty: Turning Fear and Doubt into Fuel for Brilliance*. New York: Portfolio.
- Garvey Berger, J. 2019. *Unlocking Leadership Mindtraps: How to Thrive in Complexity*. Stanford, CA: Stanford University Press.

Endnotes

1 Frone, M. 1990. "Intolerance of Ambiguity as a Moderator of the Occupational Role Stress—Strain Relationship: A Meta-Analysis." *Journal of Organizational Behavior* 11, no. 4: 309–320.

2 Caligiuri, P., and Tarique, I. 2012. "Dynamic Cross-Cultural Competencies and Global Leadership Effectiveness." *Journal of World Business* 47, no. 4: 612–622.

3 Yakhnich, L., and Ben-Zur, H. 2008. "Personal Resources, Appraisal, and Coping in the Adaptation Process of Immigrants from the Former Soviet Union." *American Journal of Orthopsychiatry* 78: 152–162.

4 Bochner, S. 1965. "Defining Intolerance of Ambiguity." *Psychological Record* 15: 393–400.

5 Budner, S. 1962. "Intolerance of Ambiguity as a Personality Variable." *Journal of Personality* 30, no 1: 29–50.

6 Based on the data we have collected through my consulting group, TASCA Global, using the Cultural Agility Self-Assessment (CASA). Please visit TASCAglobal.com for more information.

7 Roets, A., and Van Hiel, A. 2011. "Allport's Prejudiced Personality Today: Need for Closure as the Motivated Cognitive Basis of Prejudice." *Current Directions in Psychological Science* 20, no. 6: 349–354.

8 Crisp, R. J., Hutter, R.R.C., and Young, B. 2008. "When Mere Exposure Leads to Less Liking: The Incremental Threat Effect in Intergroup Contexts." *British Journal of Psychology* 100: 133–149.

9 Caligiuri, P., Mencin, A., Jayne, B., and Traylor, A. 2019. "Developing Cross-Cultural Competencies through International Corporate Volunteerism." *Journal of World Business* 54, no. 1: 14–23.

10 Traylor, A., and Caligiuri, P. 2019. "The Study Buddy Effect: Studying Abroad with a Close Friend and the Development of Cultural Agility." *Research in Comparative and International Education* 14, no. 4: 466–476.

11 Caligiuri, P., and Tarique, I. 2012. "Dynamic Cross-Cultural Competencies and Global Leadership Effectiveness." *Journal of World Business* 47: 612–622.

12 Caligiuri, P., DuBois, C.L.Z., Lundby, K., and Sinclair, E. September 2020. "Fostering International-Domestic Student Integration through an Intervention to Increase Cultural Agility." *Research in Comparative and International Education.* doi.org/10.1177%2F1745499920954311 (archived at https://perma.cc/5L7A-NTPX)

13 This is a verbatim excerpt from Ibelle, B. Winter 2017. "When in Rome, Sao Paulo, Beijing." *Northeastern University Magazine* (Winter 2016/17).

Curiosity to expand your understanding of cultural differences

03

Currently living in both Singapore and the Philippines, Ramon Segismundo is known within the industries and the communities in which he operates. His clients and peers see him as one of the most forward-thinking global human resource strategists. Providing expertise in leadership development, talent management, and business transformation, he has helped organizations and individuals deliver excellence and realize their full potential in almost every country in the world. Originally from the Philippines, Ramon has lived in the United States, the United Kingdom, and Singapore and has worked in almost every country in the world. "Before working in a country where I had never worked before, I do a lot of research on the new country's history, society, and culture. This process provides me a better understanding and appreciation of the business and its people," Ramon offered. This is Ramon's natural curiosity in action. Curiosity is a deep desire to know more about something of interest.

Even as a child, Ramon described having an insatiable passion for learning and a sense that there will always be more to know about different countries and cultures. His hobby as a young boy was geography. He was naturally drawn to maps, studying countries, their capitals, and key cities. From the maps he wanted to learn more about the place, so he researched their political leaders, their history, and the characteristics of their people. Ramon visited many countries mentally long before he set foot in them.

Ramon's insatiable curiosity for countries, societies, and cultures was strongly encouraged at home. While still in elementary school, his father and older brother encouraged him to read *National Geographic* magazine and other foreign books and publications about international affairs. This preparation and natural interest proved useful: In 1991, at age thirty-four, he went to Singapore with his family to take on an Asia-Pacific human resources role. In 2002, he was assigned to London for an international HR position responsible for emerging markets. In 2005, Collegeville, Pennsylvania, was his next stop as vice president for HR in the Asia-Pacific region.

Before moving to Singapore, the United Kingdom, and the United States, as you might expect, Ramon became a passionate student about "all things global including Singaporean, British, and American" and honed his skills for observing and asking cultural questions through respectful inquiry, so as to not offend.

For example, when his family arrived in the United States, Ramon observed something unexpected. He realized his father changed his style and was considerably more open, taking more risks, experimenting with approaches in his role, and communicating more assertively at work. His father opined that "these are the behaviors for which Americans are known. They fit with the values in this country—and I have to instill these as my own."

With his global experiences, Ramon's curiosity was redirected beyond just understanding historical facts and places on maps. He wanted to know about a culture's values, their origins, and how they manifest in daily life. Broadening his curiosity in this way was an intergenerational gift from Ramon's father that paid dividends for Ramon as a culturally agile professional later in life.

With a sincere desire to understand the values which underlie what is observed, Ramon learns more than most people do about the cultural context he is in. As a result of this deep knowledge, he can make more effective decisions in a professional context. Ramon's biggest test of his cultural agility came when working for GlaxoSmithKline as the international pharmaceuticals vice president for human resources. The geographical span in which Ramon needed to navigate was, essentially, the entire emerging market world except for the United States, the United Kingdom, and Europe.

In many ways, Ramon had been preparing for this series of roles his entire life. Along with practical knowledge, Ramon knew how to respectfully ask questions in each of the countries he worked. He began by talking with his colleagues at different organizational levels and inquired about what fosters their job success and what keeps them up at night. These two questions produced remarkable patterns within countries and important insights on how to be successful.

By listening, respectfully asking questions, observing, and respectfully asking even more questions, Ramon learned not only the business issues in the country or region but also the cross-cultural issues. This nuanced understanding of context enabled Ramon to implement human resources practices effectively within the various subsidiaries. Ramon was not the "headquarters person" who was out of touch with local realities. Rather, he was the trusted colleague who could employ cultural agility to create practices consistent with guidance from headquarters and practically actionable in each country.

Ramon was neither from headquarters nor from any given subsidiary but had the wealth of insight from both. As a respected boundary spanner, he was able to encourage GSK that many best practices could originate outside headquarters and the developed markets. In one example involving a global mega-merger, Ramon and the Asia-Pacific division were commended by headquarters for completing the organizational integration and the selection and appointment process in record time, thereby enabling the Asia-Pacific division to go beyond the merger uncertainties and focus on the business. This became a template and best practice for the rest of the world and provided Ramon the ticket to be promoted to the international HR role in London.

Ramon is now a highly sought board member, currently serving on four boards. His curiosity makes him a natural in these roles because he can ask the questions that uncover the truth, enabling boards to provide the oversight and governance necessary and empowering CEOs and senior leadership teams to be the best that they can be. Putting his wealth of knowledge to serve a broader group of firms, Ramon founded a Singapore-based management consulting, advisory, and executive coaching organization called 1-HR.X Private Limited. With a deep knowledge of global markets, he can help companies' leaders develop a business transformation plan that can be implemented globally and will enhance stakeholder value.

Applying his global skills back in his home country of the Philippines, Ramon also serves as the president and chief operating officer of the Hijo Resources Corporation. Growing from a Philippines-based company in the banana industry that started in 1969, Hijo is a group of companies with core values in entrepreneurship, stewardship, collective leadership, creativity, and innovation—with diversified businesses ranging from tourism and agriculture to property development and port operations. More recently, when Ramon's natural curiosity needed a new outlet, he pursued and completed a doctorate in business administration from the Singapore Management University. Taking a sabbatical from Hijo, Ramon is now in the final stages of a certification from the Berkeley Executive Coaching Institute.

Curiosity

Curiosity is a motivation or desire to seek and find answers. Curiosity works in our lives much like a flashlight would in a dark room. Without a flashlight in a dark room, you will trip over the coffee table, not realizing it was there. The same is true in cross-cultural situations. Having a metaphorical curiosity flashlight, you will better see and understand the situation and avoid tripping over cross-cultural coffee tables.

People who are higher in curiosity are likely to be more culturally agile because their curiosity propels them to take an active interest and engage in ways to learn about other countries and cultures. They do this naturally, directing their curiosity to research, question, and, ultimately, better understand the cultures of the people with whom they interact and the countries in which they work. The deeper and fuller their knowledge about countries and cultures, the clearer their understanding. If you have ever met a person from another country who seems to understand your country's politics, history, and geography better than you do, then you have met a culturally agile person who has a high level of curiosity.

Most of us think of ourselves as curious. Hilton, the global hospitality company, commissioned a survey of over 2,000 adults and found that over 90 percent of the survey respondents self-identified as being curious.[1] In today's information age, where we can find an answer to the most random of queries within seconds, many people believe curiosity is the same as Google searches. It is not. Googling how much to tip a taxi driver upon arrival in a new country is not an indicator of curiosity; searching for a quick answer is different from true curiosity. The quick internet search is the equivalent to cramming for a test on a subject which is only important for that brief period. It is *not* curiosity. Curiosity is a deeper, more insatiable desire to understand the unknown.

Rather than the 90 percent estimate, based on population estimates of genetic predispositions, only about 20 percent of the population has a natural propensity toward curiosity. This bears out in how we choose to spend our time and the level to which we are interested in a topic. For example, in the same Hilton survey, about half of the respondents were open to new experiences, one of the hallmarks of curious people. About half of the respondents believed that vacations should be for relaxation – and not exploration in new places and experiences. The preference for exploration is a classic behavior of a curious person.

Assess your curiosity

How curious are you? To learn more about your own level of curiosity, we can turn to the pioneering research of Drs. John Cacioppo and Richard Petty.[2] They found that people differed in their desires to think, learn, and know more, calling it one's "need for cognition." Based on this research, we can understand the behavioral patterns of people with high and low need for cognition or curiosity. Adapting some of Cacioppo and Petty's original items, the following will help you determine whether you are higher or lower in curiosity.[3]

Read each of the following seven sentences and make an X next to each sentence with which you are in strong agreement. Try not to overthink any question. Usually your first answer is your best one.

- ☐ I would prefer complex to simple problems.
- ☐ I find satisfaction in deliberating hard and for long hours.
- ☒ The idea of relying on thought to make my way to the top appeals to me.
- ☐ I prefer my life to be filled with puzzles that I must solve.
- ☒ The notion of thinking abstractly is appealing to me.
- ☐ I would prefer a task that is intellectual, difficult, and important to a task that is somewhat important but does not require much thought.
- ☐ I usually end up deliberating about issues even when they do not affect me personally.

Count the number of Xs you marked. If you have two or fewer checked, your natural curiosity and need for cognition is likely low. If you had five or more checked, it is likely high. And, if you are like most people, you had three or four checked and are somewhere in between.

Your early-life curiosity

For curious people, encountering something novel provides an opportunity for discovery, which is stimulating a pleasurable reward. Some people are born with a predisposition for appreciating and gravitating toward novelty; it is as pleasurable based on the way their bodies handle dopamine, the pleasure and reward neurotransmitter. For them, discovery in novelty is stimulating, satisfying, and energizing.

If you have naturally high level of curiosity, there are some things you likely did as a child: You might have relentlessly explored your neighborhood, possibly too far for your parents' comfort. You might have spent hours tinkering, disassembling, or dissecting. Perhaps you stayed up far too late pursuing knowledge about a given topic or spent far too much time asking and pondering questions without answers. When confronted with a difficult mental challenge, you did not lose interest in your quest to understand (that is, until it was solved and became too familiar). At that point you likely grew bored and moved on to the next topic. Your behaviors might have been maddening or amusing to your parents, depending on their appreciation of curiosity.

As you developed, depending on your family and education system, your natural curiosity was either encouraged (at one extreme) or stifled (at the other extreme). If a naturally curious child is placed in an educational system or has a family supportive of exploration, creativity, and practical application, their curiosity is rewarded and is enhanced. If that same child is placed in a family that does not appreciate questions, exploration, and experimentation or is sent to a school which rewards memorization and the unquestioning acceptance of knowledge over discovery, the child's curiosity could become dull and she could lose knowledge seeking as a source of pleasure.

Your early-life curiosity has stayed with you to some extent and has affected your relationship with curiosity today. If your curiosity was stifled, this chapter will hopefully offer some strategies to ignite a deeper need to understand cross-cultural situations.

-My curiosity has been lowered by my environment.

Types of curiosity

In adulthood, whatever your natural level of curiosity, it takes on a certain form.[4] Each of these forms of curiosity is useful and important and has its own usefulness in how you work in another country and with people from another culture.

Can you see your curiosity behaviors in one or more of these?

Broad-based knowledge seeking

The self-assessment at the start of the chapter assessed one form of curiosity: *the need for cognition*, or a basic desire for knowledge. If this is your type of curiosity, you become interested in a topic and keep researching, questioning, and learning until you have a comfortable level of understanding. You love the knowledge for the sake of knowledge, and your interests might be highly diverse—music, electronics, biology, whatever.

If you have a natural curiosity, as a culturally agile professional, you have likely already studied cultures for the pure sake of knowledge, long before there was an opportunity to work in another country or with people from different cultures. You likely learned another language without an immediate need to use it. You might know more than most people about geopolitical issues, a country's history, economies, religion, and the like.

Look into more.

Culture-specific understanding

There is another form of *curiosity which reduces uncertainty* when presented with a novel problem or challenge. Your curiosity becomes deeply stoked, well beyond the Google search, at the time when it is needed and valuable to solve a problem or address a challenge. If this is your type of curiosity, you become a diligent, passionate student responding to the situation at hand. You rise to the top of the class, so to speak, because you take the time to go deeper into the investigation than most would, even losing yourself in a state of flow trying to solve a problem or address a challenge.

As a culturally agile professional, this form of curiosity manifests once the target culture is known. At that time, you become laser-focused on meeting the cross-cultural challenge with deep knowledge and understanding. You fervently start learning the cultural nuances of the country in which you will be working, the language you will need, and the nationality of the new vendor or team members. If you will be assigned to a city for a two-year assignment, you might spend countless hours investigating the pros and cons of each neighborhood in your host city. If language skills are needed, you would begin lessons online, with a private tutor, through independent studies, and the like. You immerse yourself in the culture, reading about the country, watching documentaries, asking questions of those who know the culture, and seeking knowledge online.

Experiential novelty seeking

Novelty seeking is yet another form of curiosity. If this is your type of curiosity, you are likely intrepid and willing to take some risks to enjoy new experiences. You are propelled to try new things and go places you have not seen, meet people for the first time, and try new foods. People probably describe you as having an insatiable zest to experience all that life has to offer. You likely become bored when life becomes too routine or predictable and you probably enjoy exploring "off the beaten path" while on vacation.

As a culturally agile professional, this form of curiosity pushes you to explore more than most would. As a novelty seeker, you will arrive in a host country and just want to wander the city, meet people from the host culture, and enjoy the thrill of having the new experience. Without deliberating too much or needing full clarity (compared to what others would need), you will put your hand up to accept an international assignment, to work on a global team, or to lead a cross-cultural project. The novelty of the culture is the initial draw, and you enjoy the process of discovery. Your cross-cultural learning will happen not through preparation, but through experience.

Interpersonal understanding

The last form of curiosity is *interpersonal understanding*, a deep interest in learning about other people's lives, digging deep into what makes them tick, so to speak. If this is your type of curiosity, you enjoy learning about the people in your life or those who come into your life: what they do (and with whom), their life history, and why they do what they do, including their motivation, thoughts, desires, and values. Social media is one outlet for this, but if this is your type of curiosity, you likely want to know more about someone beyond what is curated on Facebook, LinkedIn, or Instagram.

As a culturally agile professional, your desire to learn about people will propel you to understand their values, norms, and behaviors. The more you get to know people from another culture, the more you will be able to form patterns to understand cross-cultural differences in how to communicate, collaborate, and build trust. You will learn cultural nuances firsthand.

The importance of curiosity for cultural agility

Todd Kashdan and his colleagues conducted extensive research into the behaviors exhibited by those who have a high level of natural curiosity.[5] They found that people who are naturally curious can adapt to novelty, thriving in situations of anxiety and uncertainty. They also discovered that curious people had a social ease in that they had positive emotional expressiveness, and they could comfortably use humor and be playful. They were unconventional in their thinking, enabling them to demonstrate open-mindedness by not being defensive or critical.

There are a variety of career-enhancing benefits that follow curious people. Just ask Albert Einstein, who described his success by saying, "I have no special talent. I am only passionately curious." Elevating curiosity to a virtue, Einstein offers this as a piece of career advice:

> The important thing is not to stop questioning. Curiosity has its own reason for existing. One cannot help but be in awe when he contemplates the mysteries of eternity, of life, of the marvelous structure of reality. It is enough if one tries merely to comprehend a little of this mystery every day. Never lose a holy curiosity.

While a Nobel Prize is not in everyone's future, Einstein is making an important point. Curiosity offers career-enhancing benefits, such as heightened creativity, better problem-solving, and improved relationships.

Heighten creativity and improve problem-solving

If you have a high need for cognition, you find diverse topics interesting and have researched them extensively. When faced with a problem to solve or a situation requiring creativity, your broad knowledge base enables you to combine ideas, possibly in unexpected ways, to develop a more creative solution. Culturally agile professionals are often able to integrate the best of their own culture with the best of other cultures to generate creative solutions.

Research by Lydia Hagtvedt and her colleagues found that those who used their curiosity in a targeted way were able to craft more creative solutions.[6] They will take the time to do the deep (and often time-consuming) dive into the topic and, in doing so, ultimately find a unique solution. When working in another country or with people from a different culture, this ability to focus deeply to generate a solution is particularly helpful because the solution to a problem is rarely the one that is most readily available from your own cultural lens.

Have more engaged relationships

People who are curious want to know more about people, whether they are meeting them for the first time or interacting with someone they know well. The interpersonal interest is sincere, coming from a place of genuine curiosity. That sincerity can be felt and works like an interpersonal glue holding the relationship together. After all, everyone likes to feel interesting in the eyes of others. Those who have a naturally high level of relationship building (see Chapter 6) will reap the benefit of being curious about people most naturally. As a culturally agile professional, tighter interpersonal bonds with people from different countries and cultures will give you a ready-made network of go-to cultural coaches.

Fostering curiosity for cultural understanding

If you were fortunate to have been born with a genetic predisposition for curiosity, raised in a family that reinforced your curiosity, educated in a system that allowed you to pursue cognitive interests, and chose a profession where knowledge acquisition was rewarded, then it is likely that you already have a high level of curiosity. However, if you are like most people, then you would benefit from a boost in your current level of curiosity.

Fostering curiosity, in the broadest sense, requires both *an initial interest* in the novel experience, thing, situation, or person and *an appropriate level of confidence* that the novelty is manageable.[7]

Create the initial interest

For many people, igniting curiosity needs an initial spark, something to pique one's interest. If you hear a lecture on medieval French poetry and the speaker has a passion and enthusiasm for the topic, you might be sincerely inspired to learn more. Unless you were a poetry enthusiast, independent of that gripping lecture, it is likely that you would not be curious about and engage in learning about medieval French poetry.

In the same way, we often see college students change their majors after taking just one class with a world-class expert who ignited their natural curiosity about a topic. Teachers, professors, speakers, and role models who are passionate about their topic help to foster our curiosity. Curiosity can also be sparked through an engaging documentary film, TED talk, article, or YouTube video. We need a spark to light the curiosity fire.

What sparks your interest in different countries or people from different cultures? For many people, the spark comes from something connected to something they enjoy. One of the most impressive culturally agile executives I met while working in Italy shared that, as an American, he became interested in the Italian culture after watching the 1953 movie *Roman Holiday*. Many culturally agile professionals found their initial curiosity push from reading a novel, hearing a song, or watching a movie set in another country.

I always smile when a colleague or friend, seemingly out of nowhere, starts asking me many questions about communication or trust building in a certain culture—only to later find out that the reason for the curiosity is a new romantic interest. (New relationships always have the boundless energy to fuel serious doses of motivation.) Whatever provides the kick-start for you is fine—no judgment. Cultural curiosity will meet you where you are, whatever your interests in food, sports, music, etc.

Build your confidence

Even with the passionate lecture on medieval French poetry stoking your interest, if you do not understand French, then your initial interest might quickly wane because you cannot understand what you are reading or might not have the confidence that you could learn the language quickly. You need to be able to handle the novelty—in this case French—to foster curiosity further for the topic.

Once your initial level of interest in a topic, place, or person is ignited, curiosity propels you to continue learning. Your curiosity will fan your desire to learn until you either lose interest or lose confidence in your ability to succeed in learning. In the latter case, people most often lose confidence not because of limits in their natural ability to succeed, but more often because of limiting self-talk, the unhelpful voice in our heads saying, "*It is over your head,*" "*You will never be able to learn this,*" or "*She's out of your league.*"

There are many ways to quiet any negative self-talk to increase your confidence to learn about cross-cultural situations. Here are a few:

- Focus on the novel situations in which you have succeeded, and own your strengths that helped you succeed at that time. Play through the reels in your memory of times when you successfully learned how to succeed in a new environment, starting with a new employer, meeting new friends, or working on a new team. Remind yourself that you already have the skills needed to succeed in learning about the next new environment.
- Try to identify the root of the negative self-talk to minimize its power in the current cross-cultural situation. It is likely that the negative self-talk is rooted in something from your youth or young adulthood. You are wiser and more mature now and have handled more novelty since those negative seeds were planted. Think of those self-imposed limits like grade-school shoes you have long ago outgrown. They just are not needed anymore because you are a different person with different capabilities to handle the ability to learn in any cross-cultural situation.
- Adopt a growth mindset, giving yourself permission to not understand everything perfectly at first. Perfectionism gets in the way of learning about a new cultural context. Give yourself the chance to go on a learning journey with more than a few unknown paths to explore.
- Build your resilience. Having a higher level of resilience (see chapter 4) also helps tremendously in allowing you to keep pursuing your interest in cultures, even when things go wrong. Your resilience enables you to bounce back from setbacks and stay focused on learning.

Even among people who are initially confident in their abilities to learn, I have seen them "give up" pursing an interest in cultures because the context seems too overwhelming. The classic example is the person who accepts an international assignment in another country. Prior to the start of the assignment they learn about the culture and begin to learn the language. Upon arrival, they become quickly overwhelmed when behaviors are not as predictable as the cross-cultural training made it seem, and no one understands their attempts to speak the language. With their confidence bruised, they retreat to the comfort of their compatriot community and lose interest in learning more about the host country and learning to speak the host language.

The best way to fan the embers of curiosity begins in cross-cultural situations which will be more developmental, a bit friendlier, so to speak. With many of my client organizations, we have started buddy programs where employees are hosts to the colleagues who are visiting or relocating from another country. The cultural buddies are coaches, creating a safe context in which questions can be asked and advice given about cultural nuances. Both parties are trained, the buddy and the buddied, to best learn how to ask and answer culture questions in a way that is most developmental.

Build your curiosity

As a culturally agile professional, you can actively build your curiosity by sparking initial interest in different countries and cultures. Once this initial interest is ignited, you can continually build your confidence that you can learn about and understand the new culture. Here are a few things you can start doing today to build your cultural curiosity.

Learn your natural limit for curiosity and then push it

Einstein once said, "The important thing is to not stop questioning. Curiosity has its own reason for existing." Everyone stops questioning at some point, and knowing your natural limit is an important part of building curiosity. Practice asking at least two more questions than you normally would in every situation. At home, ask two more questions when your spouse or child shares a story. At work, ask two more questions in meetings or presentations during Q&A. With colleagues, ask two more questions when they share information about their recent business trip or project. Whatever your natural limits are for asking questions, push yourself to ask two more questions. This behavior will create a habit—one that will build your natural tendency to seek more information.

-ASK MORE Q'S!

Research your interest from a different cultural perspective

Identify an interest, something you would dedicate discretionary time to investigate. This could be any broad topic that currently holds your attention—politics, fashion, food, art, music, sport, celebrities, science. Next, select a country of interest. Start investigating how your topic of interest is different in your country of interest. Within that search, identify and keep pursuing knowledge. See how far you can take your natural interests. When you think you have acquired some level of understanding, engage in a conversation with someone from the culture of interest who also enjoys the topic.

Create a goal to learn about a culture of interest

Research the business and economic landscape in a few countries as part of your professional development. These should be the countries or cultures you most need to understand for your own professional growth. You can study them by identifying the geographies or growth markets in your company. Think also of the countries that are leading in your industry or functional area. You might also select the culture of your clients, customers, or colleagues. Once you have a targeted list of a few countries, commit to investigating what makes those countries unique from the perspective of your industry or functional area (e.g., finance, engineering, marketing, journalism). Learn about the institutions which affect your target cultures—socializing agents such as history, religion, economy, political structure, legal system, and the like.

Seek to understand reasons for behaviors

If you are not naturally curious about people, try to build this skill more actively when in conversation with others. One way to do this is to, when appropriate, ask others for reasons they have made certain decisions—such as why they attended a school, selected a profession, accepted a specific job, lived in specific location, and the like. Remember, this is not an inquisition. Be sure to listen with an open mind and give the other person your full attention without judgment. Being interested in the diversity of reasons why people behave the way they do will give you practice in becoming curious about people from different cultures. It will also build your store of possible explanations for motivated behavior.

Seek to fully understand cultural challenges

Cultivate your curiosity to understand the cultural differences others have experienced. Talk to those who have worked in different countries and with people from different cultures. Ask them to describe the perceptual challenges they had when they were living abroad or working cross-culturally.

In which situations did they have the greatest challenge in interpreting an outcome? What did they do to clarify situations? What was interesting from what they shared?

Approach experiences and engage in pattern recognition

Cultivate a curiosity about cross-cultural situations. Imagine channeling your inner cultural anthropologist and continually look for patterns and possible reasons for those patterns. If you can understand the pattern, you can seek the explanation. Then, share your observations—just the facts—with someone who understands the target culture and, ideally, also understands your cultural lens. These bicultural guides are often best able to explain not only what you are seeing but the underlying cross-cultural values that have resulted in the observation.

Key takeaways

- Curiosity is the desire to seek understanding. Applied to cross-cultural settings, curiosity helps culturally agile professionals understand novel cultural environments.
- Our natural level of curiosity is a function of our genetic wiring for novelty and how much we were encouraged to pursue understanding when presented with something novel.
- Curiosity is elevated in situations when you have an initial interest in a topic.
- Curiosity accelerates when you have confidence in your ability to learn and understand the new context.
- Curiosity can be developed more broadly when you practice some behaviors, such as asking questions, looking for patterns, and seeking explanations in the culture.

Keep reading

- Dweck, C. 2012. *Mindset: How You Can Fulfill Your Potential*. London: Constable & Robinson Limited.

- Grazer, B., and Fishman, C. 2016. *A Curious Mind: The Secret to a Bigger Life*. New York: Simon & Schuster.
- Leslie, I. 2015. *Curious: The Desire to Know and Why Your Future Depends on It*. New York: Basic Books.
- Livio, M. 2018. *Why? What Makes Us Curious*. New York: Simon & Schuster.

Endnotes

1 Hilton. 2018. "New Survey Explores Link between Travel and Curiosity." https://newsroom.hilton.com/curio/news/new-survey-explores-link-between-travel-and-curiosity (archived at https://perma.cc/D6FZ-5BBW) [Accessed September 22, 2020].

2 Cacioppo, J. T., and Petty, R. E. 1982. "The Need for Cognition." *Journal of Personality and Social Psychology* 42: 116–131.

3 Cacioppo, J. T., Petty, R. E., and Kao, C. F. 1984. "The Efficient Assessment of Need for Cognition." *Journal of Personality Assessment* 48: 306–307.

4 Kashdan, T., Stiksma, M., Disabato, D., Mcknight, P., Bekier, J., Kaji, J., and Lazarus, R. 2017. "The Five-Dimensional Curiosity Scale: Capturing the Bandwidth of Curiosity and Identifying Four Unique Subgroups of Curious People." *Journal of Research in Personality* 73: 130–149.

5 Kashdan, T., Sherman, R., Yarbro, J., and Funder, D. 2013. "How Are Curious People Viewed and How Do They Behave in Social Situations? From the Perspectives of Self, Friends, Parents, and Unacquainted Observers." *Journal of Personality* 81, no. 2: 142–154.

6 Hagtvedt, L. P., Dossinger, K., Harrison, S., and Huang, L. 2019. "Curiosity Made the Cat More Creative: Specific Curiosity as a Driver of Creativity." *Organizational Behavior and Human Decision Processes* 150: 1–13.

7 Silvia, P. J. 2008. "Interest: The Curious Emotion." *Current Directions in Psychological Science* 17, no. 1: 57–60.

Resilience to cope when cultural differences produce challenges

04

Dr. Dana Born (Brigadier General, USAF Retired) has exemplified resilience, the ability to meet and overcome challenges, throughout her military, business, and academic leadership roles. As an unlikely start to her global career, Dana was born and raised in Penn Yan, New York, which, at the time, had about 2,000 residents. She recalls her first commercial air flight being the one she took to start at the US Air Force Academy in Colorado Springs, Colorado, after high school. From that day forward, Dana has not stopped flying, literally and metaphorically.

Recognized for cultural agility early in her military career, Dana became the first female US Military Exchange Officer to the Royal Australian Air Force. In 1986, at only twenty-five years of age, her three-year assignment in Melbourne, Australia, marked the first time she was ever out of the United States. Never having lived overseas, it was an eye-opening experience for Dana and one that launched her global career. "Assuming cultural similarity led to some mistakes in my first few months in Melbourne," Dana recalled.

As do most culturally agile professionals with high levels of resilience, Dana built a trusted network of host nationals in Melbourne who provided her with tangible advice and emotional support. She was able to bounce back from those initial mistakes and had the humility to learn the importance of the context from her host national counterparts. Dana's assignment was successful, and her cultural agility was noticed by the Air Force. It was clear she possessed the goal-directed optimism for other challenging international assignments, was willing to embrace multicultural challenges, and could work effectively across countries and cultures.

In 2008, Dana became one of the rare female general officers to serve in Afghanistan during Operation Enduring Freedom. When the Afghan military leaders chose to model their National Military Academy of Afghanistan (NMAA) after West Point and the Air Force Academy, Dana was selected as a mentor. While invited, this mission required a high level of cultural agility because the military culture in Afghanistan was an allegiance to people, such as the president or a tribal leader, rather than to the Afghan constitution, as would be needed in a military academy.

Working with high-ranking military leaders in Afghanistan, Dana needed to help create the educational system that would, ultimately, socialize the Afghan cadets into this new professional approach. The academy was ultimately established by 2005, Dana was there for the first graduating class in January 2009, and the academy is operating successfully to this day. In reflecting on this mission, Dana shared how she "felt honored to be an eyewitness to opening opportunities for the next generation of leaders in Afghanistan based on the shared commitment for cross-cultural learning and resilience."

Dana's resilience enabled her to succeed in these interesting cross-cultural assignments throughout her career. It did not take an assignment for her incredible strength of her resilience to become clear. It was evident on a single day—on September 11, 2001—when Dana's resilience was tested in unimaginable ways. At the time of the attacks, Dana was serving as the commander of the 11th Mission Support Squadron, Bolling Air Force Base, in Washington, DC. When the Pentagon was struck, Dana became one of the on-scene commanders in Washington, relocating the Air Force's top leaders to an alternate command post and leading rescue and recovery efforts at the Pentagon. What makes Dana's leadership on 9/11 even more remarkable was that she led the mission without knowing the fate of her two young daughters, both in the Pentagon's day care center at that time.

Even as she was unsure of her daughters' or husband's safety, Dana was able to provide emotional and tactical leadership, keeping the members of her squadron focused on the tasks of that day. It took nine hours to learn that her daughters and husband were safe. In the weeks to follow, Dana's squadron "went on a 24-hour schedule, working 12-hour shifts manning a call center and assistance office for people who had lost family members at the Pentagon. They also helped set up the process for identifying bodies and distributing benefits."[1]

Dana successfully led her squadron to excellence in that mission—a mission for which she and her command later received multiple military commendations. Her leadership enabled others to shine as well. The Air Force recognized four from her squadron for valor based on their work during that mission. Thirty more from her squadron won citations for their exemplary work and tireless effort.

That tragic day made thousands of heroes, people who showed tremendous resilience in the face of extreme trauma. Like Dana, these heroes were resilient enough to marshal the resources necessary to comfort, save lives, and serve others' needs under conditions that seemed impossible to anyone observing.

Being in command on 9/11, Dana demonstrated courage, leadership, and deep reserves of resilience. Her attributes, however, did not just appear on 9/11; they had been cultivated throughout Dana's life. They are the same attributes she honed and used to break the glass ceiling in the Air Force and institute sweeping changes at the Air Force Academy. In a long list of firsts, Dana was the first female aide to the secretary of the Air Force. She was the first female general officer during Operation Enduring Freedom. She was the first female service academy graduate general officer. She was also the first female dean of the United States Air Force Academy, where she led some of the most challenging, extensive, and positive changes in the academy's fifty-year history.

When Dana retired from the United States Air Force after thirty years of service, her stellar leadership and character had already been widely recognized. She is the recipient of the Secretary of the Air Force's Eugene M. Zuckert Award for Outstanding Management Achievement for the positive changes at the United States Air Force Academy under her leadership as dean. She is also the recipient of the Air Force Association's Hoyt S. Vandenberg Award for outstanding contributions to aerospace education, the Air Force Distinguished Service Medal, the Legion of Merit, and the Defense Meritorious Service Medal. The list of her awards could continue but the theme most important to understand is her resilience. Every award reflects Dana's willingness to accept challenging roles, excel in them, and not give in to negative emotions caused by setbacks.

Dana is currently on the faculty of the Harvard Kennedy School of Government, where she has served as the codirector for the Center for Public Leadership and is faculty chair for the Senior Executive Fellows Program, faculty advisor for the Black Family Graduate Fellowship, and lecturer in Public Policy. In these roles, Dana travels to almost every continent to lead leadership workshops and courses. Her students, leaders from all around the world and from every sector, can see that Dana not only teaches character-based global leadership, she embodies it.

When I think of resilience, I think of people like Dana. She and I went to graduate school together at Penn State University in the early 1990s. A book could be written on her accomplishments, and it would be gripping because of the challenges Dana has surmounted. As her friend, I have been able to admire (and be inspired by) Dana's grace, optimism, and emotional strength, embodying resilience at the highest level.

Resilience

Now it is your turn. Think of someone in your life you think has resilience. Who came to mind? If you are like most, you probably thought of someone who was a cancer survivor or someone who overcame childhood adversity or a great personal loss, such as the death of a spouse—or even someone like Dana who was able to execute a wartime military mission without knowing if she would ever see her daughters and husband again. The person you are thinking of likely exhibited great personal strength in the face of a challenge.

We tend to think about a person's level of resilience relative to the adversity faced as though the adversity *produced* the resilience. This is not exactly true. Resilience manifests through challenges but is not *caused by* challenges. Resilience is present before it is needed and marshaled when it is needed. It is built and honed over time, acting like an excellent insurance policy; you hope you never need it, but having it is critically important when something goes wrong.

Another common misconception of resilience is that resilient people do not feel the depth of negative emotions, such as fear, anger, or sadness. Dana experienced all those emotions on 9/11. Having an emotional response to those things that cause us distress is a natural part of being human. For resilient people, the negative emotions, while present, do not become debilitating. The way we balance our negative emotions with optimistic feelings or goal-directed responses is when our level of resilience shines.

The American Psychological Association defines *resilience* as

> the process of adapting well in the face of adversity, trauma, tragedy, threats or significant sources of stress—such as family and relationship problems, serious health problems or workplace and financial stressors... It means "bouncing back" from difficult experiences... Resilience is not a trait that people either have or do not have. It involves behaviors, thoughts and actions that can be learned and developed in anyone.[2]

Individuals respond differently when faced with adversities. Those with a higher level of resilience are better able to bounce back after setbacks, keep concerns in perspective without having them become debilitating when trying to accomplish a task, and push forward with confidence in the face of a challenge.

Your resilience enables you to cope with stressful situations in a healthier manner—and adjust after a reasonably short period of time. In this chapter we describe those behaviors and actions that bolster your resilience to make you ready for whatever challenge ahead, personally or professionally. Your goal should be to build resilience to manage challenges more positively and have it in reserve if you ever face adversity. Like that insurance policy, I hope the limits of your resilience are never tested.

Resilience as a cultural agility competency

My research has found that resilience is a critical cultural agility competency which affects your ability to successfully work in different countries and with people from different cultures. Lost baggage, lost in translation, or just simply lost, unable to find your hotel, are a few of the more minor challenges that happen when working across cultures. Resilience is a critical cultural agility competency because a greater number of unfamiliar and unpredictable situations are inherent when working in different countries and with people from different cultures. Mistakes, missteps, and challenges are far more prevalent when we are out of our comfort zone because of the cultural differences in work styles, communication patterns, national systems, and the like. When working cross-culturally, resilience enables culturally agile professionals to cope with problems, laugh off minor missteps, and keep challenges in perspective without feeling overwhelmed.

Resilience and the other self-management competencies discussed in this book are particularly important for those working in another culture because the novelty of the new culture creates stress for most people. Novel situations are unknown and unpredictable, placing our bodies under greater levels of stress, even without us really knowing it. Drs. Ingrid Anderzén and Bengt Arnetz conducted a longitudinal psychophysiological study of professionals working in their home countries compared with professionals working in foreign countries.[3] Taking blood samples to test for physiological changes in stress hormones, they wanted to examine whether living and working in the foreign environment was a natural stressor for working professionals. Their results found that during the same few years, those working in a foreign country had increases in stress hormones. They had increases in their prolactin levels and decreases in testosterone levels. These physiological responses were at their worst in the first year but remained a concern for several years in the foreign environment.

This is not the whole story though. The negative effects of living in the foreign country were mitigated when individuals had the individual characteristics necessary to adjust to life in their new country. They had the natural self-management competencies, such as resilience, to cope with the stress of living in the host country. This is not only true for the international assignees in the study; it is true for everyone working in multicultural environments. Individuals with greater resilience have less stress and better performance in cross-cultural environments.

Assess your resilience

If you are like most adults, chances are high that you have already experienced some form of failure or adversity in your personal or professional life. Difficult experiences are a natural part of life.

Reflect on the past few failures, tough experiences, or growth opportunities you have had. How did you handle them? More important, how did you recover from them? Do you believe you demonstrated a level of resilience that was higher than most? If you went through a difficult experience with others, you might have an accurate sense of your *relative* level of resilience. Compared to others, were you better able to bounce back? Or did the setback seem to affect you for a longer period?

Having an accurate self-awareness of your natural level of resilience is important for your success as a culturally agile professional. This short self-assessment was written as a first step in self-awareness, based on research on the characteristics present in those who have a high level of resilience.[4]

To get a general sense of your resilience, read each of the following seven sentences and make an X next to each sentence with which you are in strong agreement. Try not to overthink any question. Usually your first answer is your best one.

- ☒ I have high standards for myself and do not have a problem reaching them.
- ☒ My self-image is positive because my life is full of evidence that I am a capable and good person.
- ☒ Compared to most people, I set higher goals for myself and can achieve them.
- ☒ I believe one needs tenacity to be successful; most people give up before they have the chance to succeed in important things.
- ☐ I am an optimist. Pessimistic people rarely succeed.
- ☒ The failures in my life have been learning opportunities. I am better because of them.
- ☒ I have an excellent network of social support. There are people in my life in whom I confide and from whom I seek advice.

Count the number of Xs you marked. If you have two or fewer checked, your current level of resilience is likely low. If you had five or more checked, your resilience is likely high.

Behaviors influenced by your resilience

As in Dana's case, resilience is most readily visible during times of adversity. However, life provides us with numerous hints to the level of a person's resilience even before being under stress. For example, you can observe people's level of resilience when looking at how they approach or avoid stretch challenges. Before adversity or challenges are even present, the most resilient people say "yes" to accepting challenging opportunities or embracing experiences that come with some potential risk of failure.

During a stretch challenge, resilient people are more likely to have the confidence in their abilities to manage problems and setbacks that arise and be more willing to see the bright side when things do not go smoothly. They adjust well and can bounce back from setbacks. With this approach to the risk of challenges and setbacks, it is not surprising that these hardier, resilient people are generally more satisfied with work.[5]

Let us consider how resilient people manage themselves before, during, and after challenging situations, such as working in different countries or with people from different cultures.

Approaching challenges

When presented with a potential new challenging opportunity, resilient people are more likely to go for it rather than shy away from a challenge because of the risk that something might go wrong. They are more likely to engage, despite the potential personal or professional risks. Resilient people punch above their weight class, so to speak. They want to take on challenges that come with personal or professional risk—whether asking out the beautiful supermodel in the coffee shop for a date or accepting a challenging two-year international assignment. Resilient people have a greater level of optimism and tend to see challenging opportunities as goal-directed experiences.

Resilience has a strong component of optimism, but resilient people do not ignore the risks associated with the challenge. They are not naïve or blindly optimistic. They are realistic about all the potential personal and professional risks or threats associated with a given challenge but optimistic that they have what it takes to address the challenges. Resilient people are confident in their abilities to solve problems and work through life's greatest challenges. They have self-efficacy, knowing that they can address issues without personal or professional detriment.

How do you view the challenges of working internationally or in multicultural settings? Those who are higher in resilience have the self-efficacy they can succeed in unfamiliar environments. They are confident in their abilities and trust their own judgment to make the right decisions, even when the context is not fully understood. This is important because many cross-cultural situations will require you to be comfortable working in situations without familiar reinforcements or guideposts. As a culturally agile professionals with a higher level of resilience, you will be more willing to open yourself to unpredictable experiences, such as engaging with people from different cultures and working in different countries.

Managing through challenges

Challenging moments will happen, despite your best predictions for positive outcomes. In general, when people are faced with a challenge or setback, cross-cultural or otherwise, they can feel vulnerable in their inability to control the outcome. In that moment of vulnerability, negative emotions will, predictably, be felt; how we work within those negative emotions is a function of our resilience. For example, during a difficult situation, your level of resilience might affect how long you believe things will stay bad. More resilient people are quicker to see a light at the end of the tunnel whereas less resilient people see only a long, dark tunnel.

Your level of resilience will also help you understand the negative situation from the perspective of what you can control and what is out of your control. More resilient people can identify the aspects of the negative situation which they could not control; at the same time, they can admit their role in creating the negative situation. More resilient people can place blame accurately while less resilient people lose their accuracy on assigning blame—either blaming themselves or others incorrectly. This is particularly problematic in a cross-cultural context, when less resilient people are quick to point to "them" as the cause of the problem, almost always identifying the culture as the problem. The root cause is almost always cultural misperceptions.

Growing from challenges

Almost everyone who defines *resilience* will use the idea of one's ability to effectively bounce back after a setback or failure. Having a high level of resilience has even one more benefit—the ability to grow from the situation. Research by Drs. Tugade and Fredrickson found that more resilient people have the positive emotions to not only bounce back after a stressful situation but also find positive meaning from it.[6] These researchers also found that resilient individuals were, physiologically, able to rebound from stressful encounters quickly, returning more effectively to baseline levels of physiological indicators of stress. For example, after a difficult encounter, resilient people will have a faster speed of cardiovascular recovery, returning to their baseline far faster than less resilient people.

Bouncing back is not just emotional, it is physical. Psychologists call this approach to negative situations "broaden-and-build" because the positive affect of resilient individuals enables them to engage in more challenging activities and learn and grow their personal resources through negative situations.

Higher resilience also gives people the ability to understand negative situations through the eyes of empathy and understanding, where appropriate.

In a cross-cultural context, having the ability to see situations through multiple perspectives is an important growth opportunity, especially for culturally agile professionals who are developing their perspective taking (more on that in Chapter 7).

Build your resilience

Resilience is a combination of your stable personality traits, your coping strategies, and behaviors you can use to increase your resilience.

Understand the role of your personality traits

Before we discuss the ways to build resilience, we need to examine the link between how we are hardwired and the resilience we have. As with some of the other competencies, understanding your resilience means you need to understand a bit about your genetic code.

You might remember from the tolerance of ambiguity chapter that a portion of our expressed personality traits are rooted in our DNA. As noted in previous chapters, research has found that between 30 and 50 percent of individuals' personality traits can have a heritable component. This means that at least a portion of our natural responses—our personality traits—are hardwired.

Related to resilience, your genes affect (1) whether you tend to initiate challenges some might view as stressful and (2) how you react once you are faced with a challenge that has the potential to produce anxiety. In terms of seeking out multicultural challenges, you have probably observed a natural variation among the people you know: Some friends could easily backpack around the world without a map or a schedule while others seem stressed when visiting a neighboring city. Part of the difference you observe among your friends is explained by polymorphisms in the D4 dopamine receptor gene. Variants around this gene affect whether challenges are considered pleasurable or stressful—and whether we are naturally motivated to seek challenges in the first place.

Once faced with a challenge, variants on our 5-HTTLPR gene relate to serotonin transporters, which, among its many roles, can affect how we sense our environment and feel anxiety. The serotonin transporter gene has been linked to whether we attend to positive signals—and avoid negative signals—in the environment. Variants in this gene can also affect whether we respond to situations with a greater level of optimism—affecting our willingness to work harder because we believe the goal is achievable.

If you scored extremely high on the self-assessment—and have a naturally high level of resilience—you just might need to thank those responsible for your genetic code. They have set up a springboard for your cultural agility.

Your genes might contribute to how you sense and feel stress but they are just one of the factors affecting your resilience. There are many ways to become more resilient and cope more effectively with the stressors inherent when working in cross-cultural settings.

Build a repertoire of coping strategies

Resilient people have a full repertoire of positive coping strategies. Coping strategies are the thoughts you have or actions you take to manage the stressors, challenges, anxieties, or demands in your life. You likely have some go-to coping strategies that you use all day long, such as using humor to lighten the mood when conversations are tense or going for a run at the end of long day. You might take deep breaths, call a friend, or grab a margarita. They are all coping strategies of some sort—but not all coping strategies are equally good in every situation. Research has found that any of these strategies have their place in healthy responses to stressful events, depending on the situation. The two general categories of coping strategies are problem-focused coping and emotion- or symptom-focused coping.

In the case of international assignees, the need for coping is particularly high as the stressors involved in living abroad become too difficult for many. The outcome of this heightened stress among international assignees is alarming. Research by Drs. Truman, Sharar, and Pompe found that expatriates are at a higher risk for mental health and substance use disorders, compared to their domestic counterparts.[7] They found that three times as many expatriates identified that they were feeling trapped and depressed compared to a matched set of professionals working in their home country. Too often the notion of living abroad is glamorized, without an adequate understanding of the personal and professional challenges associated with living and working abroad. As a result, individuals who do not have the full set of coping strategies struggle to adjust.

If you have not yet started to work in a cross-cultural context, begin practicing a wider variety of coping strategies and reflect on whether your challenges require an improvement in *action* (problem-focused coping) or an improvement in *feelings* (emotion-focused coping).

If you are currently in a cross-cultural work context, I encourage you to become cognizant of your coping strategies and assess whether they are appropriately placating a symptom—or merely avoiding the problem that needs to be solved. In many work settings—including cross-cultural work settings—using emotion- or symptom-focused coping exclusively in the absence of any problem-focused strategies can lead to less successful outcomes because they prevent solutions in and thwart learning from the cultural environment.

coping strategies: working out, praying, parents

Problem-focused coping strategies

If you engage in problem-focused coping you are working to manage or reduce the source of the stressor. Problem-focused coping strategies help you make a tangible or action-oriented change to improve the stressful situation. Examples of when problem-focused coping strategies are helpful are when you need to replace your clunker car, get out of a dead-end job, get into better shape after a health scare, or learn the language of your host country to speak to your host-nation colleagues. In each of these cases, doing something about the problem is better than dealing with the negative emotions associated with the problem.

There are times when action-oriented, problem-focused strategies will not be appropriate; usually in situations where you erroneously believe you can control the outcome when in fact you cannot. In this case, working to solve a problem and failing might cause greater stress because it was not yours to solve in the first place. An example is when one partner is trying to save a marriage while the other is speaking to a divorce attorney or when an employee is working toward a promotion that was already promised to the friend of the manager. Some stressful things are out of our control.

However, there are many ways we can control problems that arise when working across countries and cultures. For culturally agile professionals, examples of problem-focused coping strategies include:

- Speaking to a cultural coach for advice on how to best present material to a host national client before interacting in a cross-cultural situation
- Proactively researching cross-cultural issues that might become trip wires during interactions
- Setting work meetings at a time that will work with your time zone, so you are not waking up in the middle of the night for calls and meetings
- Building a close network of go-to colleagues from different cultures who can help you navigate cultural challenges

- Becoming comfortable asking host national colleagues when you need advice on how things are done in their country

Emotion-focused coping strategies

Emotion-focused coping strategies help you manage how you feel about the stressful situation without trying to directly control or solve the problem. These coping strategies help you manage the symptoms and regulate the stressful feelings resulting from the negative situation. Seeking support from a colleague after a difficult meeting is an example of emotion-focused coping. If that same colleague can give tangible advice on how to address the concern, then the strategy is double-counted; it is also a problem-focused strategy. Extra points.

For culturally agile professionals, examples of emotion-focused coping strategies include:

- Exercising while traveling to get your endorphins pumping
- Engaging in a pleasurable activity that reflects the host country (e.g., take in a museum or sporting event)
- Visiting a park, taking it in as part of the cultural experience
- Taking a favorite book or music to enjoy while you travel
- Experiencing massage or yoga in a new location
- Spending time with compatriots, ideally those who can help you better understand the cross-cultural situation you are in

Do you know your tendencies for coping strategies? Think about the past most stressful events in your life. What do you do when under stress? Some people confront the stressor directly to mitigate the negative effect or make the best of the situation while others turn to alcohol, complaining, or other outlets to placate their stress symptoms. Cross-cultural situations, especially international assignments, can trigger whatever approach you naturally use. Be sure you practice the more positive coping strategies before engaging in significant cross-cultural experiences.

Seek support to increase resilience

Everyone can build their resilience by mastering the problem-focused and emotion-focused coping strategies described in the previous section; they will help when in a stressful cross-cultural situation. As a culturally agile professional, you can also build resilience by seeking support from others. Positive, supportive relationships, whether family, friends, or coworkers, will buffer the effects of stress and foster increased resilience. For some people, this relationship-based support can be felt during participation in more organized groups, such as a community volleyball league, a quilting class, a prayer group, or a book club.

Whether in structured or unstructured ways, as you develop cultural agility, it will be important for you to build your network of positive, culturally agile colleagues. Surround yourself with colleagues who are successful in cross-cultural settings. They can help guide you to a greater level of success. Accepting their help and support will strengthen your resilience. Remember to include colleagues who are enthusiastic and successful with their cross-cultural work. Ask them about their challenges and their strategies for coping with those challenges. Avoid those who view cross-cultural work as being rife with insurmountable challenges or seem to be adversarial with people from other cultures.

Positive affect can be delightfully contagious and can provide you with an extra boost of resiliency. Just as you are surrounding yourself with positive people to guide you, try being a cultural coach or buddy to someone who is unfamiliar with your culture. The act of helping others can also be a buffer for your own stress as you experience the "helper's high," a surge of feel-good endorphins.

It is also helpful to learn from the challenges you have faced. To this end, it is helpful to conduct cross-cultural premortem and postmortem analyses with your those in your network, especially biculturals. Biculturals who understand both your culture and the culture in which you are working will be able to identify the challenges and offer realistic interpretations of the experiences. If you bring them in before the cross-cultural experience, they can help you see some of the challenges you might experience (the premortem). They can also help you understand situations when they do not go so well with a more culturally accurate lens (the postmortem).

Practice stress management techniques

Practice some techniques to manage stress while working in another country, even during business travel. There are many stress management techniques you can try. Three of the most often suggested are:

- The frequent expression of gratitude to help with cognitive reframing and focusing on the positive side of situations

↳ Be thankful

- Improving your physical health to ease your body's response to stress
- Practicing meditation or mindfulness to become more attuned to the present and your authentic responses to stressors

Keep challenges in perspective

There are few certainties in life, other than death and taxes. That said, I am relatively certain that you have faced some form of adversity, an unwanted change, or an unexpected stressor in your life. Unwelcome things happen that are out of our control. How we respond to them is a function of our resilience.

When challenges happen, it is important to keep both the problem and the steps you make toward resolution in perspective. For some stressful problems, it helps to focus on the better possible outcome once the initial stressor has passed. In a sense, this means finding reasons to be optimistic and training your brain to enjoy what positive things might be in the future. For example, if you are going through a divorce, you could focus your optimism on how the future might be improved once you are in a better relationship or once you are able to enjoy the freedom that comes with being single. Doing this will help you keep the current problem in perspective of your broader future and replace dread with optimism.

You can also keep stressful challenges in perspective by identifying the things we can control and focusing on the small steps toward addressing bigger challenges. For example, if not being understood in a host country is stressful for you, accept that your language skills are not yet fluent enough to be understood by host nationals. Instead of giving up or becoming anxious at the thought of speaking a new language, reframe the goal. Start with small polite interactions with clerks and neighbors, celebrating the "wins" along the way. Try to learn a small number of new words each day. Focusing on small steps within your control will put stressors in perspective and build your resilience.

Be good to yourself

As mentioned in the section on emotion-focused coping, there are ways to be good to yourself, especially when stressful events are out of your control. Being good to yourself includes having the ability to recognize how you have grown from stressful events in your life. The American Psychological

Association reported that many people who have experienced tragedies and hardship have reported better relationships, greater sense of strength even while feeling vulnerable, increased sense of self-worth, a more developed spirituality, and heightened appreciation for life.[8] In doing this positive self-reflection, you can also increase your self-efficacy and confidence in your ability to handle the adversities that you might face in the future.

Being good to yourself also means being good to your body by eating healthy foods, getting enough sleep, and exercising. It also means engaging in activities that you find relaxing, such as meditation, yoga, massage, a nature walk, and the like. All of these can be easily ignored when you are working in other countries but try to budget the time for them.

Remember that when working in a cross-cultural setting, things will likely go wrong from time to time. As a culturally agile person, try to keep the stressful situations in perspective and feel emboldened by your resilience. The cultural environment is new, and you are in a learning mode. As my students would say, "You've got this." If you are looking for more tips on how to build resilience, I recommend reading the American Psychological Association guide to fostering resilience.[9]

Key takeaways

- Resilient people are more likely to engage in stretch challenges, such as international assignments, because they believe they have the confidence and goal-directed optimism to work through potential problems that will inevitably arise.
- Resilience is one's ability to bounce back, emotionally and physically, after problems and adversity.
- Your current level of resilience is a combination of personality traits, coping strategies, and experience in marshaling resources when needed.
- Resilience can be developed without suffering through significant adversity. Adversity tests resilience, but resilience is present or absent prior to a person needing it during a difficult situation.
- Cross-cultural situations require resilience because there is a greater level of unpredictability and risk for mistakes when working in different countries and with people from different cultures.

Keep reading

- Brown, B. 2017. *Rising Strong: How the Ability to Reset Transforms the Way We Live, Love, Parent, and Lead*. New York: Random House.
- Duckworth, A. 2016. *Grit: The Power of Passion and Perseverance*. New York: Scribner.
- Graham, L. 2018. *Resilience: Powerful Practices for Bouncing Back from Disappointment, Difficulty, and Even Disaster*. Novato, CA: New World Library.
- Sandberg, S., and Grant, A. 2017. *Option B: Facing Adversity, Building Resilience, and Finding Joy*. New York: Knopf.
- Southwick, S. M., and Charney, D. S. 2012. *Resilience: The Science of Mastering Life's Greatest Challenges*. Cambridge: Cambridge University Press.

Endnotes

1 Munsey, C. 2007. "Women Leaders: Brig. Gen. Dana H. Born, PhD, Air Force Brigadier General and Air Force Academy Dean of the Faculty." *Monitor on Psychology* 38, no. 7: 79.

2 American Psychological Association. 2018. "The Road to Resilience," https://www.apa.org/topics/resilience (archived at https://perma.cc/EB7H-BPBJ) [Accessed July 27, 2020].

3 Anderzén, I., and Arnetz, B. B. 1997. "Psychophysiological Reactions during the First Year of a Foreign Assignment: Results of a Controlled Longitudinal Study." *Work & Stress* 11, no 4: 304–318.

4 Connor, K., and Davidson, J. 2003. "Development of a New Resilience Scale: The Connor-Davidson Resilience Scale (CD-RISC)." *Depression and Anxiety* 18, no. 2: 76–82.

5 Cash, M. L., and Gardner, D. 2011. Cognitive Hardiness, Appraisal, and Coping: Comparing Two Transactional Models." *Journal of Managerial Psychology* 26, no. 8: 646–664.

6 Tugade, M. M., and Fredrickson, B. L. 2004. "Resilient Individuals Use Positive Emotions to Bounce Back from Negative Emotional Experiences." *Journal of Personality and Social Psychology* 86, no. 22: 320–333.

7 Truman, S. D., Sharar, D. A., and Pompe, J. C. 2011. "The Mental Health Status of Expatriate versus U.S. Domestic Workers." *International Journal of Mental Health* 40, no. 4: 3–18.

8 American Psychological Association, "The Road to Resilience."

9 American Psychological Association, "The Road to Resilience."

PART TWO
Relationship-management competencies

Have you ever been shopping and asked a fellow customer or the clerk for a recommendation on an item for which you had little familiarity? Or have you tried a new restaurant and sought the advice on what to order from an online app or the waiter? Maybe you asked a trusted neighbor for a recommendation on a contractor, dog sitter, or physician? If you are like most people, you have had one of these experiences where you looked to others for advice in the face of uncertainty. In unfamiliar situations, it is natural for us to look for clarity through others.

Culturally agile professionals who have *relationship-management competencies* are better able to reduce the ambiguity and learn to the norms of the cross-cultural context through our connections with others. The next three chapters cover how you can build your relationship-management competencies: humility, relationship building, and perspective taking.

Humility, covered in Chapter 5, focuses on how to express to the cross-cultural environment that you respect the nuances of the cultural context and seek advice. Cultural humility recognizes the important role the environment can play in your ability to be successful. Chapter 6 discusses how to build the skills for effective relationship building cross-culturally. Culturally agile professionals with a high level of relationship building can form meaningful connections with others, irrespective of their culture. In Chapter 7 we discuss how to build your cultural agility competency of perspective taking. Perspective taking is the ability to see situations from multiple perspectives and interpret behaviors correctly in the given context.

Each of these three competencies, unlike the competencies in Part One, has some cultural nuances. This means that to effectively use these relationship-management competencies, you will need *both* the behaviors inherent in the competency and the ability to adapt those behaviors to align with culturally appropriate norms. When engaged effectively, these three competencies can propel your success in any new context. As a culturally agile professional, they will enable you to learn from the environment, garner the support needed, and foster a trusted network to accelerate success in any cross-cultural situation.

Humility to learn from others who are culturally different from you

05

As a facial plastic and reconstructive surgeon at Harvard Medical School, Dr. David Shaye has a busy Boston practice of aesthetic and reconstructive surgery. David performs facelifts, nose jobs, and eyelid and brow lifts in a posh office overlooking the Charles River. For many months a year, however, David lives in Africa, operating, teaching, and conducting research on surgical delivery in low-resource settings.

David has taught and performed surgery in Zimbabwe, Rwanda, Malawi, Bhutan, Dominica, Guatemala, Nigeria, and Nepal. In many developing countries, a birth defect or deformity can be a stigma with life-altering implications. In these regions of the world, parents of children with a visible deformity can feel guilt and anger, and this can affect employment or marriage. With surgical care, people with a birth defect or deformity can become fully integrated back into society. There is a renewal of hope.

David is quick to point out that there are many talented and dedicated surgeons in these countries, but not enough of them. For this reason, he focuses on surgical education. He is teaching at Rwanda's Central University Teaching Hospital of Kigali, working with Rwandan students, surgeon trainees, and faculty. "I am there to teach but in fact I have learned much more. I am a better surgeon because of my experience in Africa, which presents challenging problems with few tools," he said. "I am part of a team of Rwandan surgeons," said David. When treating a patient with a complex problem, David and his Rwandan colleagues decide what must be done and the essentials needed to accomplish the task. They put their heads together to be innovative. David described an example of an infant born with a lymphatic malformation (a cyst the size of a basketball in the neck). In the United States, there are expensive medicines prepared in pharmacies that can be injected as treatment, none of which is available in Rwanda. Working with what was available, David and his Rwandan colleagues found an available and inexpensive pill form of one of the important medicines used in the injection. They crushed the pill, mixed it by hand to dissolve it, and injected it, after which the deformity disappeared entirely. They repeated this approach on ten other children and published the results. All the children had near total resolution of their cystic deformity, at a cost of four cents per child in medication. This was an example of cultural integration combined with local knowledge of what was available and possible in the local community.

By consistently needing to innovate and think outside the box in Rwanda, David's creativity grew as surgeon, which has benefited his Boston-based practice. He notes that "plastic surgery is built on creativity. There is a lot of cross pollination. When you are thinking of how to do a certain surgery with limited instruments, limited time, limited medicine, your mind is always challenged. This pushes the surgical mind outside of the comfort zone, and it's a good state to be in for a facial plastic surgeon." David is using his growth mindset to broaden and build his skills as a surgeon.

Working in Africa has also helped David broaden his understanding of what challenges surgeons face around the world. In a single day of clinic in Rwanda, David can see more challenges than he would see through the entire year of his Boston-based practice. He explained that "surgical problems in Africa can be immense, both in quantity and quality. Diseases that would be caught and treated early in the United States are ignored because of poverty and a lack of trained surgeons and supplies." While David focuses on training surgeons to address these issues, he emphasizes that while teaching, he also learns a great deal.

The context of a patient is critical to improving his or her care, and there is no way of understanding that context unless you defer to local expertise. As a culturally agile professional, David knows the value of the local surgeons, as they have a wealth of knowledge and understanding of their home context.

To illustrate the importance of local knowledge, David gave the example of solving the problem in Nepal of the far distances patients and their families need to travel to receive care. "Distance is a major hurdle to overcome in Nepal. It is not uncommon for patients from remote areas to walk several days on foot, then travel by bus for a few days to see a surgeon." Partnering with a Nepali surgeon who understood this challenge deeply, a creative solution was developed. David and his Nepali colleague taught a small group of "surgical scouts," laypeople who were trained to identify cleft lips and palates, to seek out those needing surgical care. The surgical scouts then trekked through the most remote areas of Nepal for five months, identifying patients and scheduling them for surgery in regional hospitals. Once patients were scheduled, the Nepali doctors would travel to the regional hospitals to perform the surgeries. Searching for those who need care and identifying how they can access care took a deep understanding of the local context, along with some collaboration-based creativity.

The same issue of how to reach patients needed a different solution in Zimbabwe. Again, local knowledge made all the difference. David observed that, despite how impoverished patients and their families were when they arrived at the government-sponsored hospital, they each had a cell phone. Working with mobile phone service providers, team leaders, and local experts, a plan was crafted to reach more patients. This time, rather than trekking scouts, they sent text messages to inform the population how and when those with cleft lips and palates could be treated. The campaign was wildly successful. David said that "most people who showed up that year heard about us through our text messaging campaign." Technology and local knowledge can be leveraged in many settings to improve care.

Cultural understanding—and a willingness to try a different way of doing things—was critical for reaching patients, but it is also critical for patient care. For example, knowing that his American communication style might not be the best approach for interacting with patients, David used his humility to learn the culturally appropriate way to build trust and show empathy. He learned this by observing, asking questions, asking for feedback, and modeling his Rwandan colleague, a fellow surgeon and trusted friend. "Learning the culturally appropriate way to build rapport, discuss consent, and break difficult news to patients helped me tremendously," he said, adding, "while we always aim for the best surgical result, much of treating a patient lies in compassion and understanding. As Dr. Francis Peabody said, 'The secret of caring for the patient is caring for the patient.'" To accomplish this critical task, listening, learning, and adapting to the local norms was essential.

Even the technical aspects of performing surgery requires cultural knowledge. As an example, David shared that Nigerian surgeons taught him how some facial scars are intentional marks of beauty within certain Nigerian tribes. While not as widely practiced today, scarification, which was used to identify family lineage, can also be used to hide surgical incisions. This was a skill the Nigerian surgeons were able to teach David.

David Shaye has a high level of cultural humility. He, like all global professionals with cultural humility, is open to learning from those who have a different cultural lens, see the contextual limits of their knowledge, and enthusiastically seek advice and feedback from others on how to succeed in that context.

David is a culturally agile physician but credits this to his earliest life experiences and a combination of both nurture and nature. David grew up in Nepal. His parents, both working with Save the Children, gave David both the developmental experience of living in another country and a deep respect for other cultures, to feel comfortable in novelty, tolerate ambiguity, and approach every new context with a curiosity to learn. Today, David and his wife, Jessica, whom he met in Zimbabwe, replicate the gift that David's parents gave him by relocating their three young daughters to Rwanda each year for three months.

Humility

Humility, as a dispositional trait, has received a bad reputation over the years because it has been equated to low self-esteem, a lack of confidence, and low self-worth. This could not be further from the truth. Humility is just the opposite, in fact. Humble professionals, like Dr. David Shaye, have a strong sense of confidence in their abilities, which enables them to be willing to reach further, to comfortably test their assumptions, and to recognize that their understanding might not apply to the local context.

Humility enables people to learn from others. People who are humble can comfortably ask questions, show vulnerability, and receive feedback without having these diminish their self-esteem or accomplishments.

Cultural agile professionals use their humility from a position of strength, not weakness. They can seek the advice from others as an exercise in understanding without appearing needy or insecure. They actively project authenticity, that they are open to others' thoughts, feelings, and opinions. They can appear more confident—and not weak—when admitting they do not know something. For this reason, they are highly respected because they do not let their egos get in the way of truth.

Research has found that humble professionals have four important responses that are present across a variety of professional and intellectual situations.[1]

1 They are not ego-involved when it comes to their knowledge and expertise. This means they do not feel threatened in the presence of someone with more knowledge and expertise. They can, concurrently, embrace opportunities to learn from others without having their confidence diminished.
2 They can change their minds and revise their views if a strong alternate case is presented. To do this they must admit, if only privately, that their initial opinion, choice, or perception was wrong.
3 They have a healthy respect for another person's lens, even if their values and beliefs are different. Their perspectives might remain fixed, but they do not feel threatened or insulted by another person's divergent views. Being in a state of disagreement or seeing the world through different lenses does not limit a humble person's ability to interact with that person; they can discern and respect people whose character is good and intentions are just.
4 Lastly, they are willing to question their assumptions and test the limits of their knowledge. They do not have a low self-worth; rather, they value their understanding such that they do not assume they have all the answers. They embrace opportunities to learn and grow.

Assess your humility

Having an accurate self-awareness of your level of humility is important for your success as a culturally agile professional. This short self-assessment was written as a first step in self-awareness. The assessment is based on the extensive research on intellectual humility by Elizabeth Krumrei-Mancuso and Steven Rouse.[2]

To get a general sense of your humility, read each of the following eight sentences and make an X next to each sentence with which you are in strong agreement. When considering each item, be honest with yourself and try not to overthink any question. Usually your first answer is your best one. Choose the response that best describes your attitude or feeling about each statement. Please select the response that comes to mind first when you read the statement.

- ☐ When someone disagrees with one of my ideas, I do not take it personally. Also, I am usually surprised when others do take professional or intellectual disagreements personally.
- ☐ I do not feel anger or resentment when someone disagrees with me in the context of a professional disagreement or intellectual discussion. Disagreement is a normal part of professional conversations.
- ☐ I have changed my mind about a topic when I hear compelling evidence that is contrary to what I originally thought was true.
- ☐ It is easy for me to admit that I was incorrect in my judgment when I find out more information contrary to what I initially thought was true.
- ☐ It is easy for me to be friends with those who have different values (e.g., political, religious) from my own.
- ☐ I enjoy engaging in conversations with people who have different opinions, even when I know neither of us will change our minds.
- ☐ The times when I most believe I am right are the times when I most want people to question my decisions. I do not like to mistake the strength of my belief with the truth about something.

Count the number of Xs you marked. If you have two or fewer checked, your humility is likely low. If you had five or more checked, your humility is likely high. And if you are like most people, you had three or four checked and your perspective taking is somewhere in between.

Humility as a cultural agility competency

Culturally agile professionals need cultural humility because it enables them to be open to feedback and learning from those who are different from themselves. They see the contextual limits of their knowledge and seek advice from others. As a result, they are more successful in their cross-cultural roles. Studies have found that global professionals who are higher in cultural humility are more effective in their multicultural and international roles because they gain the confidence and trust of others and are not perceived as arrogant or ethnocentric.

Those who have cultural humility receive more feedback and support from those in their cross-cultural work environments compared to their ethnocentric colleagues. Ethnocentric professionals, on the contrary, have been shown to be less effective because they approach their international and cross-cultural roles with the belief that they need to impart "their ways" onto those from other cultures. Some of the most stunning, costly, and embarrassing mistakes in international business were made because business professionals opted for solutions that were familiar and known over solutions that were generated by those from different cultures.

Studies have also found that chief executive officers with a higher level of humility had top management teams who were better able to collaborate, share information and a vision, and make joint decisions.[3] You do not need to be the CEO to reap the benefits of humility. Those with higher humility:

- are more effective leaders
- are viewed as more trustworthy
- foster learning-orientation in their teams
- experience an increase their team members' engagement and empowerment

When using humility as a cultural agility competency, there are two issues to consider. The first is how to effectively express humility in different cultural contexts; the second is how the cultural context can impose challenges on the development of humility.

Cultural differences in the expression of humility

More than any other cross-cultural competency, how you express your humility is just as important as the humility that is in your heart. In a study I conducted with Nataliya Baytalskaya and Mila Lazarova, we found that professionals needed both *felt* humility and *culturally appropriate expressed* humility to be culturally agile.[4] What one culture might view as an expression of humility, another culture might view as rude or weak. Let us consider the following two examples:

> **Tara:** The first culturally agile professional, Tara, comes from the Netherlands, a country which is known to have a more direct communication style. In direct communication cultures, like Tara's home country, words are spoken with no implied meaning. When Tara asks questions, she asks them directly. Her direct communication style of asking questions shows engagement when she is interacting with those who are also from direct communication cultures like she is. However, Tara's direct communication style could be misconstrued as rude or arrogant when with colleagues from indirect communication cultures. In indirect cultures, more would be read into the question, including the reason

for the question, the tone of the voice, and the situation in which it is asked. Tara, despite her sincere interest, might be interpreted as having *the opposite* of cultural humility, even if her intention had been to humbly seek understanding.

Tad: The second culturally agile professional, Tad, comes from Thailand, a culture with an indirect communication style. In indirect communication cultures, people interpret more from the context in which communication occurs, such as tone, facial expressions, and body language. Communication, in these cultures, is far more subtle. Tad would likely learn from the environment by observing and modeling behavior. He might be less likely to ask questions openly but might make more subtle observations to see if context can be explained. He believes he is acting with humility, but in a direct communication culture, his silence might be viewed as indifference or lacking interest.

The good news for well-meaning culturally agile professionals like Tara and Tad is that these communication differences can be learned and practiced and mastered over time. Once your communication repertoire is built, you can use the culturally appropriate way to express your felt humility successfully in any culture.

Contextual challenges for developing cultural humility

There are some contextual trends that, when ignored, can make humility a difficult cultural agility competency to develop in a business environment. In many cultures around the world, even in more collectivist, group-oriented cultures, we are seeing trends that are *fostering* self-centered hubris. Consider some of these global forces operating *against* the development of humility:

- Social media encourages us to broadcast our every move while search engines place us into our own data bubbles, isolating us from diversity of ideas.
- Thinking of others over oneself is becoming more difficult when individuals are competing for limited resources—good jobs, seats in the best colleges, and promotions.
- Cultures traditionally more collectivistic are becoming progressively more self-centered in younger generations, making it more difficult to foster humility.

Developing cultural humility—in the face of the social pressures of today—is significant. At the same time, skills can be learned to help increase humility. These are discussed in the next section.

Developing humility

Humility is a cognitive and motivational competency, which means you can learn to think and behave with cultural humility—and, in turn, reap the rewards of doing so. Unlike some of the other cultural agility competencies, there is no genetic component to humility. You are not hardwired to be predisposed to humility. You gain humility through your values, experiences, and behaviors.

In a study I conducted with Victoria DiSanto, we looked at newly minted global MBAs who were selected for elite leadership rotational programs in three leading global organizations, one each from the financial services, pharmaceuticals, and consumer products industries.[5] They were graduates of the world's leading global MBA programs, many were multilingual—60 percent were fluent in two languages—and all were well traveled.

Across the companies, the rotational programs were structured the same way: Each participant had three rotations, one of which would be an international assignment lasting from six to twelve months. At the time of the study, the groups were evenly staggered: One-third was on their international rotation, one-third had not yet started their international rotation, and one-third had completed their international rotation. On the face of it, one could assume that the participants in this study were already culturally agile. When the data were analyzed, however, a different picture emerged.

The participants were asked to self-rate both their knowledge and their abilities to conduct business in another country. This was the surprise: The group who had not yet been on their international assignment rotation rated themselves significantly *higher* than the other two groups in terms of their ability to work in a cross-cultural environment. The group who were currently on the international rotation and the group who had already completed it both rated their abilities lower in comparison.

With hubris, the participants assumed that their combination of international travels and multicultural contacts with classmates had endowed them with a high level of cultural agility. When the veil of the academic setting was lifted, they were shocked to realize that their cross-cultural abilities were not as advanced as they had thought. Cultural bravado was replaced by cultural humility.

Some people learn humility quickly from some powerful situation that taught them a life lesson, like the MBAs in our study did while on their international rotation. You do not need to be humbled by cross-cultural situations to build cultural humility. Just the opposite: Your cultural humility can help you be successful in cross-cultural work environments and avoid embarrassing or "humbling" mistakes.

Humility is easier to develop than many of the other competencies and can be practiced long before you are working in another country or with people from another culture. To develop humility, you need to master three developmental processes: increased self-awareness, understanding the influence of the cultural context on your role, and having a growth mindset.

Increase self-awareness

People with a high level of self-awareness understand themselves, their strengths and weaknesses, their abilities and blind spots, and the situations where they are at their best and their worst. They can accurately perceive how they will react, respond, and perform in various situations. Self-awareness can be emotional, cognitive, perceptual, and even physical. For example, if you need to reach something on a top shelf and you can accurately predict whether you need a step stool, then you have self-awareness about your reach. If you need to give a presentation and you accurately know how much practice you need to be successful, then you have an accurate self-awareness about your oratory skills. If you are visiting your mother-in-law and you know you will become agitated when she talks about your parenting style, then you have an accurate understanding of your emotional response.

Get to know yourself at a deep level before you start working in a cross-cultural context. Three of the most common techniques to build self-awareness include:

- Reflect on the situations or moments when you were at your best, the situations when you had the greatest sense of pride, or the circumstances under which you go into a state of flow, when the demands meet your skill level and you lose yourself in whatever activity you are engaging in. Through this type of self-reflection, you can identify your strengths, traits, and competencies and enhance your understanding about the situations which will bring out the best in you.
- Becoming more in touch with yourself through a meditation practice will help to process your emotional reactions with heightened self-awareness. Several apps can kickstart a meditation practice, such as Calm.com.
- Many people shy away from seeking feedback because they do not want to be vulnerable to others who are aware of their weaknesses. If you have

a person or people in your life with whom you can feel safe, ask for (and really listen to) their feedback.

Understand the contextual limits of your abilities

No matter how brilliant someone might be in their chosen profession, they still need to learn how to be successful in the given cultural context. Even if your tasks are fully rooted in the hard sciences, you will need to perform those tasks in a context of a socialized environment. This is important and often overlooked among professionals with significant technical expertise, such as engineers, physicians, or finance experts; they tend to overemphasize the universality of the laws of physics, biology, and mathematics and ignore the context in which their expertise is applied.

Unless you work in full isolation, your job involves people, whether clients, patients, colleagues, collaborators, students, or teammates, who compose the cultural environment in which your work is accomplished. For example, as a university professor, I need to understand the norms for the classroom in any culture where I teach. As a physician, Dr. David Shaye, who was profiled at the start of this chapter, needs to understand the factors affecting patient care.

Learning how the cultural context will influence success within your profession is nuanced. As a place to start, ask yourself:

- What are the situations where I need to gain credibility, earn trust, and communicate clearly to be effective? What is the culturally appropriate way I accomplish this aspect of my job?
- Are there tangible differences in the culture that will influence how work is accomplished (e.g., laws, political systems, regulatory agencies)? How can I learn about these?
- Are my skills and abilities contextually bound such that they would not apply in another cultural context? How can I test my assumptions about this?
- What are the situations in which I need informational, instrumental, or emotional support from others to be effective? How can I foster support-giving in others in this cultural context?

Increase your growth mindset

As a culturally agile professional, Having a growth mindset will be fundamental to your success as a culturally agile professional, because it will enable you to use humility in order to learn from those who understand the culture without a fear of failure. You replace the risk of failure with the desire to learn. Stanford psychologist Carol Dweck uncovered the difference between a growth mindset and a fixed mindset. She defines these mindsets as follows:

> Individuals who believe their talents can be developed (through hard work, good strategies, and input from others) have a growth mindset. They tend to achieve more than those with a more fixed mindset (those who believe their talents are innate gifts). This is because they worry less about looking smart and they put more energy into learning.[6]

As Henry Ford famously said, "Whether you think you can, or you think you can't—you're right." To foster cultural humility, a growth mindset to learn in the context is critical. If you are embarrassed to take a risk and try to be successful in the host country, your ability to learn the context would be thwarted. To succeed, you will need to admit that there are contextual limits of your knowledge, request support from others, and be open to making mistakes as you learn.

Build your cultural humility

Once the foundation is set for you to use humility, there are ways to continue practicing the competency. Here are some suggestions for behavioral changes you can start making today.

Practice asking for assistance

To learn from those in the cross-cultural environment, you need to have the skill to ask for help to build your understanding—while keeping your self-esteem intact. It will feel foreign, no pun intended, to ask for help and advice in another culture if this is not part of your regular behavioral repertoire. Recognizing that others have knowledge, skills, and abilities that could help you does not diminish your ability or contribution. In fact, you are the sage one who knows how to achieve a better outcome by harnessing the talents of others. Practice with a question, such as "Since you have deeper experience in [context], do you have any insight on…?"

Learn to praise

Praising others enables you to recognize that others have some knowledge, skill, or ability that complements your own. This will be particularly important in a cultural context because, by definition, others will know more about how to succeed in the host culture. Practice offering sincere praise for others' contextual understanding, such as "Your ability to present to such a mixed audience at that conference was impressive. I liked how you..." Be specific and authentic when you offer praise.

Show appreciation

Actively showing appreciation for others' role in your success is a skill that enables you to learn to share credit without diminishing your own accomplishments. Using a more generous communication of gratitude will foster an ability to acknowledge when and how others contribute to your success. Over time, you will see that being successful and showing gratitude for others' role in your success are not mutually exclusive. This ability will be helpful when you are in another cultural context and can more comfortably let others in as cultural coaches—and appreciate their role in helping you succeed.

Acknowledge your mistakes, if appropriate

As you become more successful, you can be caught in a trap of needing to believe you have all the answers. Having the ability to comfortably share your mistakes and how you learned from them has two benefits. First, others will view you as more authentic and transparent. Second, you will be able to admit in a cross-cultural context when your lack of knowledge caused an error or mistake on your part. By sharing your own past mistakes, you can remind yourself of your own limits while modeling humility for those you lead. Sharing mistakes is a culturally bound skill, though. Learn how to do this appropriately in the culture in which you are working so you do not make yourself seem weak.

Ask feedback-fostering questions

One simple question can be the most comfortable way to receive feedback after any professional activity. Ask a person you trust, someone who has your best interests at heart, to observe you in a work context that he or she understands very well. Then ask: "How do you think I could have been even more effective in this meeting, presentation, etc.?" The question conveys your confidence but balances it with your honest interest in improving and receiving feedback. If this one question becomes a habit, it will be easier for you to remember to ask it in cross-cultural situations when accurate appraisal of your performance will be more difficult to assess. The caveat: You need to want to hear the answer.

Ask questions about the role of the cultural context

To do this you will need to identify a few professional colleagues from different cultures. These individuals are your go-to cultural guides—knowledgeable friends and colleagues who understand one of your target cultures and can share insights, interpret situations, provide background, and the like. It is always better to have multiple guides from each culture of interest so as not to rely on just one person's opinion. An example of a question to ask your cultural guide is something like "I have never worked with clients from [culture]. Do you think I should change my style to…?

Learn something from someone junior to you

Allow yourself to be open and willing to make mistakes as you learn from those who, either on an organizational chart or a calendar, are your juniors. As a practiced act, you can start to learn that your expertise is not diminished by making mistakes and trying something that is unfamiliar. Sometimes our pride or fear of making mistakes stands in the way of immersing ourselves in cultural experiences.

Key takeaways

- Humility is a personal attribute which enables people to learn from others. People who are humble can comfortably ask questions, show vulnerability, and receive feedback without having these diminish their self-esteem or accomplishments.
- When culturally agile professionals apply their cultural humility, they can recognize the limits of their knowledge, comfortably test their assumptions, and ask for advice on how to succeed in the local context.

- Humility is an important cross-cultural competency because it accelerates success by uncovering the cultural challenges you might never see.
- There is a difference between felt and expressed humility. Felt humility is the internal belief of oneself as a humble person. Expressed humility is the extent to which others see you as a humble person. Learning how to express humility in the cultural context in which you are working is important.
- It is important to understand the extent to which knowledge, skills, and abilities are contextually bound.
- To develop humility, three developmental processes are needed: increased self-awareness, understanding the influence of your cultural context, and having a growth mindset.

Keep reading

- Black, B., and Hughes, S. 2017. *Ego Free Leadership: Ending the Unconscious Habits That Hijack Your Business*. Austin, TX: Greenleaf Book Group Press.
- Hess, E. D., Ludwig, K., and Crowe, A. 2017. *Humility Is the New Smart: Rethinking Human Excellence in the Smart Machine Age:* Oakland, CA: Berrett-Koehler.
- Kerr, A. 2017. *The Humility Imperative: Why the Humble Leader Wins in an Age of Ego*. Morrisville, NC: Lulu Publishing Services.
- Patterson, K., Grenny, J., McMillan, R., and Switzler A. 2012. *Crucial Conversations: Tools for Talking When the Stakes Are High*. New York: McGraw Hill.

Endnotes

1 Krumrei-Mancuso, E., and Rouse, S. 2016. "The Development and Validation of the Comprehensive Intellectual Humility Scale." *Journal of Personality Assessment* 98, no. 2: 209–221.

2 Krumrei-Mancuso and Rouse, "The Development and Validation of the Comprehensive Intellectual Humility Scale."

3 Ou, A. Y., Waldman, D. A., and Peterson, S. J. 2018. "Do Humble CEOs Matter? An Examination of CEO Humility and Firm Outcomes." *Journal of Management*

44, no. 3: 1147–1173. https://doi.org/10.1177/0149206315604187 (archived at https://perma.cc/6AMR-55FX)

4 Caligiuri, P., Baytalskaya, N., and Lazarova, M. 2016. "Cultural Humility and Low Ethnocentrism as Facilitators of Expatriate Performance." *Journal of Global Mobility* 4, no. 1: 4–17.

5 Caligiuri, P. M., and DiSanto, V. 2001. "Global Competence: What Is It—and Can It Be Developed Through Global Assignments?" *Human Resource Planning Journal* 24, no. 3: 27–38.

6 Dweck, C. 2016. "What Having a 'Growth Mindset' Actually Means." *Harvard Business Review*. January 13. hbr.org/2016/01/what-having-a-growth-mindset-actually-means (archived at https://perma.cc/MS92-AWZY).

Relationship building to expand your professional network across cultures

06

Euan Air is a global thought leader in the security industry who has been extraordinarily successful in planning and delivering innovative and business-friendly security solutions in multiple countries around the world. Born in Scotland, Euan was in the British Army for ten years until 1992, when he relocated to the United States for four years before obtaining his master's degree, specializing in Iranian state-sponsored terrorism.

Seeing the Middle East as a fascinating region with a rich history and tremendous professional opportunities, he moved in 2000 to Dubai in the United Arab Emirates. Still in Dubai today, Euan is now the regional security manager for Facebook in the Europe, Middle East, and Africa region. In this capacity, Euan helps to protect Facebook's people, assets, and reputation in a region spanning 116 countries with over 200 spoken languages.

Before joining Facebook, Euan had been the director of safety and security at Careem (a Middle East and North African–based billion-dollar ride-hailing provider, like Uber or Lyft, with 700,000 drivers). Euan shared that "even the definition of safety and security differs from country to country." Reflecting on his experience at Careem, Euan shared how "people, broadly, in the Middle East tend not to be directly rule followers but, rather, rule interpreters." He added the example that in Beirut, "traffic lights can be viewed, at best, as suggestions rather than a rule and the wearing of a safety belt in some Middle Eastern and African countries is a sign of personal weakness, whereas in the UAE traffic laws are strictly enforced."

Euan shared an interesting example of a situation when a Careem driver was being accused of sexually harassing American women who were visiting the historical site in Jerash, Jordan. The accusation was escalated to the US Embassy, and Euan needed to intervene to understand the case. The driver, who had an exemplary record with Careem, had, in fact, followed these two women as they walked around the historical site. This act of following them felt like stalking to these women. The Jordanian driver, surprised by the accusation, shared that he was merely ensuring that they were safe. Euan quickly realized what had happened, based on his cultural knowledge of Jordanian hospitality and honor code to those deemed to be guests. The driver's intentions were, in his mind, noble and protective. Needing more information, Euan asked the local police to wait to arrest the driver (an action that Careem would have fully supported, given its zero tolerance of sexual harassment). After a thorough investigation, Euan's suspicions were correct. The driver viewed these tourists as guests and, as he had done for others in the past, he felt a sense of obligation to ensure their safety.

Once Euan reframed the driver's behaviors to the American tourists, the women recognized how they had misconstrued his actions. They dropped the charges. Euan, for his part, added a new lesson on stalking behaviors during driver training.

Navigating these cultural nuances to create region-wide safety and security standards took Euan's extraordinarily high level of cultural agility. The result was that Careem became the region's safest form of vehicular transportation—with credit going to Euan's cultural agility.

Along with Euan's deep experiential and functional knowledge of the Middle East, he had a prescient *ability to build relationships* with people from different cultures, enabling him to form meaningful and trusting interpersonal connections with others.

Euan's ability to build relationships was shaped from his early childhood experiences. When Euan was growing up in Scotland, his parents frequently had house guests from different countries, people with whom Euan engaged enthusiastically, asking many questions about their home countries and their travels and listening to their stories of their experiences outside of Scotland.

One house guest shared a story which provided Euan an enduring lesson. This house guest, a fellow Scot, recalled a situation when he inadvertently caused a minor three-vehicle crash when he was in what was then Palestine after World War II. One car was driven by men who were Jewish Holocaust survivors of Eastern European descent, and one car was driven by Arab men. Tensions from the incident were running high and quickly approaching a physical confrontation when, out of blue, one of the passengers started talking about football. Like a release on a pressure valve, the animosity was redirected to an amicable topic (they all, fortuitously, shared a passion for the same team). The conversation continued over dinner, and a relationship formed that endured for decades. The power of the story stayed with Euan: Always look for the common thread to begin a basic sense of trust. He shared, "I like meeting people and recognize that I subconsciously strive to find commonality, to find what makes them tick, what their levers are and figure out how we can mutualize goals."

Euan also underscored the importance of knowledge when forming relationships. For example, he always learns some basic phrases in the language of the host country, wherever he is working. He also studies the host country's history because "the conversation topics which recognize national, state, or regional achievements are almost always very well received because my ability to recognize them shows my respect and interest in the area." Euan also ensures that he knows the topics to be avoided, which, almost everywhere, include religion and politics.

Euan's high level of relationship building has a natural behavioral component as well. He noted that "to make others comfortable with me, I will adapt my behaviors to better fit the image they are expecting of me." For example: I will engage with someone from, say, northern Nigeria and someone from its southern commercial capital, Lagos, very differently. I never realized I was doing this—it was all subconscious—until one evening in Karachi, Pakistan, when I was having dinner with a very experienced hostage negotiator (we were negotiating the release [thankfully successfully] of a kidnap victim), and he described me as a natural "mirror"—someone who adjusts their posture, tone, and mannerisms to reflect the person they are engaging. Monitoring myself, I recognized that to quickly gain trust, I will naturally hunch down when speaking with someone shorter, keep eye contact, tilt my head to the side or forward to show interest ("doglike", as the hostage negotiator described it!), smile, and keep my voice steady and slow. These adjusted mannerisms speak to my conversationalist's subconscious as I search and probe for the lowest common denominator, that click, that common ground, and I expand from there.

In addition to the desire to find commonality, learn about the region, and change behaviors, Euan said he uses humor, respect, and humility to foster trust and added that "my approach is guided by my belief that trust is binary and fundamental to any relationship—and that we all have an instinct to trust or not when we meet people." With this approach, he feels as comfortable in and confident of being able to manage unpredictable situations in Gaza or Riyadh as he is in a Hezbollah-affiliated neighborhood in Beirut.

In an example (which was been tailor-made for a Hollywood action movie), Euan shared a story of the time when he best leveraged his relationship building skills—with a Lebanon-based arms dealer! At that time, the black-market price of a Kalashnikov assault weapon, Euan found, was a reliable indicator of geopolitical sentiment, effectively monitoring whether there was trouble brewing in the region. Euan's "Kalashnikov Index" became a go-to indicator in the Middle East for many years. The challenge in creating this index was getting reliable data, which required forming relationships with arms dealers, not generally known for their trusting spirit. Euan did just that. (Having heard many stories of culturally agile professionals over the years, I am not easily impressed. This one impressed me.) One arms dealer even nicknamed Euan his "Muzungu brother," a term borrowed from East Africa describing a person of European descent, and noted that he just trusted that Euan would not reveal his source.

At Facebook, Euan has found an environment that is very well suited to his relationship building skills where developing relationships and collaboration, individually and with teams, is strongly encouraged and actively developed. Before joining the company, he was advised to prioritize relationship building and learning the unique Facebook culture. (After building relationships with arms dealers, this should be simple.) However, he joined just one week before the Covid-19 social distancing began in Dubai and everyone started working from home. In a vastly different format, but one so critical for culturally agile professionals today, Euan now builds relationships virtually through Portal, Facebook's smart video device.

Relationship building

People with a high level of relationship building, like Euan, will actively seek opportunities to form meaningful interpersonal connections with others. They can form positive interpersonal relationships and be engaged with the people with whom they interact because they have the skills to comfortably bond with those they meet. They are likable. They are invited to and included in a greater number of personal and professional social activities and interactions, including pre-meeting small talk, lunches, and after-work social activities. Equally important, effective relationship builders say "yes" and are more likely to *accept* these invitations because they tend to enjoy the opportunities to socialize, even when the context is unfamiliar.

As a cultural agility competency, relationship building increases cultural understanding, fosters social support, and strengthens the professional network.

Increase your cultural understanding

Learning about culture happens through interactions and experiences. For those who can effectively engage in relationship building in cross-cultural or multicultural settings, the increased number of interactions increases the chances to learn about different values, beliefs, and behaviors. These interactions also provide culturally agile professionals with more opportunities to observe and model how to behave in the different context, whether starting in a new job, joining a new team, or moving to a new city or a different country. Relationship building helps you "fit in" in any new context.

Increase your social support

Better cross-cultural relationships also mean you are more likely to be offered support because others sincerely like you and want to see you happy and successful. This support might be practical and informational (e.g., "Here's the number for tech support for assistance with your global team meeting," "Be sure to order bagels for your morning meeting or no one will attend," or "Here is the address of the best farmers' market in town."). Or the support might be tangible and instrumental (e.g., "I'll be on the call for your global team meeting in case you have any questions," "I'll pick up bagels for tomorrow's meeting," or "Let's go to the market together so I can show you how to bargain."). With the support of those who understand the context well, the faster your adjustment, the greater your comfort, and the more effective you will be in that context.

Build a wider network

Culturally agile professionals who are effective relationship builders are also better able to expand their network of colleagues across cultural and national boundaries, and this wider network has both immediate and longer-term benefits for your career. When Kristina Mäkelä and Vesa Suutari studied global careers, they asked former international assignees to talk about the relationships they had formed while abroad, people who were in their professional networks even today.[1] One global leader, reflecting on the contacts made while working abroad, noted that the cross-cultural network has helped "get things done much easier and quicker. You know who to talk to when you need information." Another former international assignee shared that the "benefit of your network is that you can find things out in a day that would normally take months." As a culturally agile professional, your expanded multicultural network can continue to enhance your career.

Assess your relationship building

Do you know how well you build relationships? Having an accurate self-awareness is important for your development and success as a culturally agile professional. This short self-assessment was written as a first step in self-awareness and is based on the research conducted by Ivy Nielsen and her colleagues on workplace friendship.[2] These researchers identified how the prevalence of workplace friendship is important, underscoring the role of workplace friendships in individuals' job satisfaction and organizational commitment.

To get a general sense of your relationship building in the workplace to date, think about your current or most recent job. With that job in mind, read each of the following seven sentences and make an X next to each sentence which you believe describes your friends at work. Try not to overthink any question. Usually your first answer is your best one.

- ☐ I have formed strong friendships with my colleagues at work.
- ☐ My coworkers and I will do things together socially outside of the workplace.
- ☐ I know my coworkers support me and would help me if I was in need.
- ☐ I enjoy my social interactions with my coworkers.
- ☐ I have a deep trust in many of my coworkers and know I can confide in them.
- ☐ I look forward to work because it gives me the chance to see (or at least interact with) my coworkers.
- ☐ One of the most important benefits of my job is that I can honestly say I work with true friends.

Now repeat the exercise above for three to five different situations that had the *potential* for interpersonal interactions, not including family or those whom you knew prior to the situation (e.g., another job, the first year of a new school, joining a new gym, moving to a new neighborhood, renting a new apartment). You can go back as far as you would like to complete the exercise, substituting "classmates/neighbors/etc." for "coworkers" and "school/neighborhood/etc." for "job."

Did a pattern emerge across this exercise? Did you form strong and lasting friendships in every new context—or only in some? If you tend to form enduring friendships from almost every new context you have experienced, you likely have a naturally high level of relationship building.

Personality and relationship building

A component of relationship building is based on natural, immutable personality traits, like the other competencies described in this book. Compared to the other competency "ingredients," such as behaviors and skills, personality is more immutable. We are stuck with our personalities, so to speak. In the case of relationship building, our brains, wired a certain way to process reward, satisfaction, and positive emotions, either approach or avoid new relationships. For some of us, meeting new people and spending time with people we do not know well are pleasure inducing and rewarding. For others, these meetings and interactions are stressful and anxiety producing. Most of us are somewhere in between, depending on how we have been hardwired in the genetic lottery.

If you are lower in relationship building, you might have a naturally lower level of the personality traits of extraversion and openness. Extraversion is one's innate desire to engage with and establish new interpersonal relationships with others. For natural extraverts, interactions with others are a source of stimulation and energy. Openness, the other affiliating personality trait, is one's receptivity to engage in novel situations, whether interactions with new people or engaging in new experiences. Individuals with a higher level of natural openness and extraversion will have less stress from new social experiences compared to individuals who are introverted and less open. The presence (or absence) of extraversion and openness accelerates (or impedes) the social interactions that help positive, engaging relationships form.

Since we humans are social animals, the more naturally social among us reap certain socially-oriented professional benefits. For example, in a research study I conducted, I found that international assignees who had the personality traits of extraversion and openness gravitated toward host national interactions and more easily adjusted to living in the host country.[3] In another study in a college setting, my colleagues and I found that students' openness affected the extent to which they engaged with students of different cultures. The same positive benefits can be found in the domestic context: A meta-analysis to determine the importance of extraversion at work found that the sociability aspect of extraversion is positively associated with leadership, a situation where social skills are needed.[4]

As a natural introvert, I found my own research results a bit depressing. Admittedly, Netflix at home will always have a greater draw than a networking event, even though I know only the latter will advance my career. The good news for my fellow introverts is that research has found that introverts may become more "socialized extraverts" as their job demands require social engagement at a more senior level of management.[5] In other words, introverts can learn, with practice, how to appear more social at work. I sure did. My colleagues, clients, and students are usually shocked to learn I am a natural introvert. With all the benefits of affiliating personality traits, people who are lower in extraversion and openness can learn the behaviors and build the skills needed to become great relationship builders.

Behaviors to foster your relationship building

There are some universal behaviors that help to accelerate how you connect with other people. If you master the behaviors of (1) increasing others' recognition of you (by increasing proximity, frequency, and duration of interactions), (2) finding similarity, and (3) using positive, engaging conversation, you will be better able to foster relationships in any new context. For an example of how these behaviors can be used to build cultural agility, please see the section in this chapter entitled "Case in Point: A Program to Foster Relationships across Cultures."

Increase proximity, frequency, duration of interactions

Did you ever hear someone say, "I cannot believe how lucky I was to move into a neighborhood (or apartment/dorm room/new office) where my neighbor (or roommate/office mate) ended up becoming my best friends. How lucky is that?" Luck was only part of the equation in the formation of that close relationship. According to research, social bonds are created using a somewhat predictable formula based on neuroscience: our brains trust those who are recognizable and familiar.[6] The formula includes having regular proximity to a person (e.g., sharing an office, an elevator, a break room, or a coffee shop), having frequent interactions (e.g., seeing the person predictably in the mailroom, coffee shop, lunch room, or gym), having interactions that are increasingly longer in duration (e.g., over time moving from a glance to a smile to a "Hi" to a comment on the weather to "How was your weekend?"). If the trusting relationship will eventually take hold, increasingly more meaningful interactions will ensue over time. Try using proximity, frequency, and duration to launch a relationship the next time you are in a new situation.

Find similarity

When we talk about cultural agility, many people immediately believe that they need to better understand how cultures differ through programs such as cross-cultural training. While cross-cultural training programs are pervasive, the focus on understanding cross-cultural differences obscures the more important behavior of culturally agile people: learning how to quickly find similarities. As social beings, we want to sense that we are alike, from the same "tribe" so to speak. That tribe could be a shared interest in a sport or hobby, a shared preference in a type of food or car, a shared reality such as having children of the same age or elderly parents, or being from the same generation with shared experiences (e.g., coming of age in the 1980s).

Whenever I start a keynote or presentation (especially one where I do not know much about the audience), I tell a not-too-personal story that will reveal my age, family status, and a few other universal demographic insights. My goal for doing this is to provide enough information for many audience members to find at least one thing on which I seem relatable, some way in which we are similar. Cultural differences become second to your perceived similarities when forming relationships.

If you are new to a company, city, or country, join a local group, club, religious community, etc.—any activity that is something that you enjoy or represents one of your values. Engaging in a shared interest or activity is one of the easiest ways to connect with people from different cultures. If your organization, community, or school has clubs of interest to you, select one with the greatest cultural diversity among the members. This will enable you to share experiences while getting to know people who are demographically different. Over the years, I have coached successful global professionals who, years later, still have "go to" wine bars, dance classes, or running clubs in different cities around the world. They can find their "tribe" in multiple locations around the world.

Without ever leaving home, you can practice finding similarity with those from different cultures. For example, if you have a sincere interest in a specific culture, join an affinity group for your culture of interest. (The best affinity groups in organizations are open to anyone and not limited to those of a single demographic category.) Attend meetings and activities with the only goals being to listen, understand, and learn—while practicing your skill at finding similarities.

Use positive engaging communication

Most people know about *active listening*, giving the person who is speaking your undivided and undistracted attention. Effective active listeners can observe and understand not only the words being communicated but also the tone, body language, and context that make up the meaning of the message. They can reflect accurately that message back to the speaker so the speaker has a deep sense that the listener really did fully understand what he or she was trying to say. Like all the skills in this section, active listening is a practiced act.

In addition to active listening, also engage in *active responding* to be viewed as a positive, engaging communicator. Relationships are built on the positive emotional response we give each other when communicating. In many cultures, this means that you care enough about what someone is conveying to you to ask a question and show your genuine interest, especially when someone starts opening up to you on a personal or emotional level. Questions that begin with "Tell me more about…" or "What was it like to…" or "How did it feel when…" are examples of lead-ins for active responding. In the cultural sense, it is always good to follow the other person's comfort with self-disclosure; if your follow-up question leads to a nonresponse or signs of discomfort, do not push with any more questions or you will seem overly intrusive.

Are you able to tell if you are having positive engaging communications with someone from another culture? For many, this is sometimes difficult to tell because the way in which positive relationships are communicated can vary dramatically across cultures. For example, many Americans will smile when they are engaged in positive communications; this is not true among those from cultures where smiles are reserved for moments of happiness with loved ones.

While there are many cultural nuances in how relationships are formed, the good news is that there are also some universal, subconscious reflexive behaviors that exist to signal that you are starting to build rapport, the precursor to trust for relationship building. These include:

- *Leaning forward:* One way to tell that the person with whom you are communicating is engaged is that he or she will lean slightly in your direction. While the amount of the body lean will vary across cultures, you should be able to see some change when the person becomes more engaged.
- *Tilting the head:* When someone is engaged with you in conversation, you will also notice a reflexive response that a person's head will tilt (sometimes ever so slightly).
- *Making brief eye contact:* Universally, brief eye contact (about the amount of time it takes to register a person's eye color) is an indication of connection. In conversation, the length of sustained eye contact will vary dramatically across cultures. The brief flash of eye contact, however, is universally accepted.
- *Removing barriers:* If there are notebooks, mobile phones, coffee mugs, and the like. between you and the person with whom you are speaking, these barriers will reflexively be moved to engage in conversation.
- *Mirroring:* Another reflexive behavior of those engaging in positive conversations is mirroring. When mirroring happens, those in conversation are adapting the posture, stance, and body position of each other. The more you are mirrored, the better the rapport.

Case in point: a program to foster relationships across cultures

Prior to the coronavirus pandemic in 2020, there were over 1 million international students studying in the United States, roughly 500,000 in the United Kingdom, and about 350,000 in Australia. The percentage of students who study abroad each year is also increasing. For example, about 350,000 Americans studied abroad in the last academic year.

The massive number of students having opportunities to build relationships with classmates from different cultures *should have* made this generation the most culturally agile in history.

Unfortunately, this has not happened. Only 21 percent of employers rate new college graduates as being culturally agile and having global and multicultural fluency, the graduates' lowest-rated competency.[7] Given this gap, it is important for universities to ensure their students are building cultural agility from the multicultural campuses on which they are studying. Universities, like many organizations, will point to diversity as a sign that people are integrating. Untrue. Merely sharing classes and some team projects is not enough to foster relationships.

One known issue impeding the development of cultural agility is the lack of friendships formed between domestic and international students. Only a small percentage of international students graduate having domestic friends. This is a missed opportunity for all students, both international and domestic, one which universities should be clamoring to solve.

My colleagues and I at TASCA Global developed a program that leverages the accelerators of relationships to increase students' cultural agility based on the four features to foster relationships with people from different cultures: start early, focus on similarities, create social ease, and meet regularly.

Start early

The first feature of the program is to start as early as possible when the students arrive on campus. For everyone, anxiety-producing situations (such as starting university in another country) foster affiliation between people. When we experience heightened anxiety, friendship bonds form quickly as a palliative way to ease the anxiety. We bond over our shared stress. The best time to start an international—domestic student integration program is during students' first semester on campus.

Focus on similarities

The second feature of the program is to encourage conversations between international and domestic students about their similarities, enabling them to identify what they have in common. Many well-meaning diversity programs exist on campus to help students appreciate differences; however, to foster student integration and the development of cultural agility, the first focus needs to be conversations around similarities. As students find similarities, the comfortable self-disclosure of interests helps to ease anxiety, increase liking, and, for some, foster friendships.

Create social ease

The next feature of this program is to provide the domestic and international students with a structured context that will make it easy to have conversations without adding social anxiety. Open social activities, such as networking events and mixers, can produce social anxiety, which only makes students retreat to the comfort of their compatriot classmates. Our program gave the students a list of questions to ask each other and provided some guidance on active listening and other conversational skills.

Meet regularly

As already discussed in this chapter, relationships form from familiarity, which requires proximity, increased frequency of interactions, longer duration of those interactions, and a greater intensity of those interactions. The last feature of our program was required regularly scheduled meetings between domestic and international conversation partners. Regular meetings occurred most naturally when embedded in a semester-long course. The students were asked to meet every few weeks with a new set of questions to ask each other (i.e., the assignments). These conversation assignments had a series of questions the partners would ask each other, along with the requirement to answer the question each time "What do we have in common"?

This program has worked in every situation and has been validated. When compared to the control group, the international and domestic students who participated in this program had better relationships, which fostered their sense of belonging and social support on campus.[8] The science of relationship formation works, which helps build cultural agility.

Cross-cultural issues affecting your ability to build relationships

There are some aspects of relationship building that are universal and others that are culturally bound. When working in another country or with people from different cultures, you will need to consult with colleagues, mentors, and friends who understand the culture. At the most basic level, you will need to understand the importance of relationships in your ability to succeed with those from a different culture. At the more advanced level, you will need to understand the cultural nuances of how those relationships are fostered.

Cultural differences in the importance of relationships

In some cultures, the strength of relationships indicates the trustworthiness of business associates. In these cultures, your ability to build relationships can make or break your ability to succeed. If you are in a relationship-oriented culture, you might observe family members or lifelong friends occupying key positions in an organization. In cultures with a lower relationship orientation, this same practice would be viewed negatively as nepotism or favoritism.

In high relationship-oriented cultures, building relationships affects how much time you will need to spend socializing, building rapport, engaging others within the network, and the like. For example, in a study conducted by Nealia Bruning and her colleagues, international assignees who were working in China had better overall work performance when they had stronger ties with Chinese national colleagues.[9] The need for this relationship building competency is especially important in cultures, like China, in which relationships are critical to building trust and credibility. One of the study participants described that, in China, you need to build relationships such that those working together are "friendly enough to want to do business with each other."

Cultural differences in how relationships are formed

This book would be several thousand pages long if I were to try to cover every known cultural difference in interpersonal communication and relationship formation. To provide some guidance, I highlight a few of the more salient and observable differences you might experience. Each can affect how you perceive others and how they perceive you as you foster relationships. The list is not exhaustive. Please consult with colleagues, mentors, and friends who understand the culture on how to build rapport, gain trust, and communicate. You can also visit MyGiide.com for more information.

Greetings

We all have been socialized on how to greet, whether with a kiss (once, twice, three, or four times; lips or cheek; real or air), a bow (how low and with whom), or a handshake (grasp tightness; double- or single-handed; number of pumps). In the US, a firm handshake and a toothy smile is the norm. In Italy and France, a double kiss is more appropriate. In Iran, men might greet other men with a kiss or handshake—and women kiss women. In Japan and Korea, bowing is more common. Greetings matter because our initial greeting sets the tone for the conversation.

Conversational distance

Think of the last time someone stood too close or too far from you when they spoke to you. Without any thought, you reflexively moved back or closer depending on your socialized norm. It was a subconscious judgment resulting in an automatic behavior. If the person moved closer or further again (using his or her automatic behavior), the subconscious action became a conscious violation. You might judge the person to be "creepy" or "weird" —or just different, depending on how much time you have spent with those from a different culture. A study of social distance in forty-two countries found that preferred distances vary considerably depending on the country.[10] For example, in China the preferred distance to stand from a stranger is about 110 centimeters whereas it is only 90 centimeters in Spain.

Conversational touching

As with greetings and social distance, there was a wide range across cultures in how much people use touch in conversation. In some countries, it is a norm to touch another person's arm for emphasis, to foster connection, or to show empathy. A study of European countries illustrates the many differences in conversational touching.[11] In Greece, for example, 32 percent of conversations included some form of touch whereas in the Netherlands it was only 4 percent.

Silence

Do you remember the last time you were in a conversation with someone who either remained silent when you were expecting a verbal response or interrupted you when you were talking? In either case, your sense of conversation flow was disrupted. The use of both silence and interruption has vastly different meanings, depending on the cultures. At one extreme, in some Latin cultures, talking over another person (i.e., interrupting) is a way to express enthusiastic engagement for what is being said. At the other extreme, in some Asian cultures, remaining silent before speaking is a way to show thoughtful engagement. When silence is used correctly in multicultural interactions, those interacting go into a state of conversational flow, experiencing a greater sense of belonging, social connection, and consensus. Without conversational flow, people can feel rejected and negative toward the others.[12] Wherever you are on this continuum, your speech pattern can affect how you will be viewed as a conversational partner.

Self-disclosure

Have you ever met someone for the first time while on a plane, bus, or in line at the market, and, without inquiry, he or she begins to tell you something you thought was too personal? What is your reaction? If you are like most, it is to get away from the person as quickly as possible (if doing so does not require a parachute). What is deemed too personal, however, differs across cultures. In some cultures, as in the United States, self-disclosing personal information about family, health, and work is comfortable. In other cultures, personal information is limited to a small circle of loved ones and therapists.

In their outstanding book on cross-cultural differences, *Riding the Waves of Culture*, Fons Trompenaars and Charles Hampden-Turner make a distinction between peach versus coconut cultures.[13] People socialized in peach cultures, like many Americans and Brazilians, are warm and fuzzy with everyone they meet. They use informal speech and are more open to self-disclosure, even during interactions with new acquaintances. Trying to break into the inner circle of relationships—the peach pit—is much harder, but it is among that smaller group that deep and lasting relationships are formed. To peach cultures, those from coconut cultures, like many Russians and Germans, seem cold and difficult to get to know. Coconuts share little if any personal information; this is reserved for close friends and family. For coconuts, unlike peaches, the bonds of friendship, once formed, are strong and enduring. It might take longer to build a relationship with a coconut, but the time invested is worth it since the relationships, once formed, will last.

Develop the ability to build relationships

As a culturally agile professional, you can foster your ability to build relationships by trying these activities.

- Expand your professional circle. While on a business trip in another country or when starting a project with colleagues from a different culture, practice the culturally appropriate ways to build rapport, gain trust, and communicate effectively. When possible, engage in culturally appropriate social activities.
- Practice understanding accents. If English is the lingua franca in your organization, you can improve your ability to understand those speaking with accented English. Practice watching movies and TV shows with actors speaking accented English. If your ear has difficulty settling into the actors' accents, turn on the closed captioning. Over time you will not need the subtitles because your ear will become accustomed to different cadences and tonality.
- Join a recreational sports team or social club in which some teammates or club members are from diverse cultures.
- Identify your trusted cross-national peers and cultivate those relationships to provide each other with cultural co-coaching. You can exchange both language lessons and cultural advice. Do things together socially, perhaps alternating cultural experiences (e.g., you invite an Indian friend to an American football game; then you go to a cricket match with your Indian friend).

Key takeaways

- Relationship building as a cultural agility competency is the ability to form meaningful interpersonal connections with people from different cultural backgrounds.
- Relationship building helps increase cultural understanding, foster greater social support in a new context, and strengthen the professional network that spans boundaries.
- Personality traits (extraversion and openness) and behaviors and skills (social skills, empathy, and active communication) are the ingredients of relationship building.

- Certain behaviors will increase relationship building, including in any new context: (1) increasing others' recognition of you (by increasing proximity, frequency, and duration of interactions), (2) finding similarity, and (3) using positive, engaging conversation.
- There are universal behaviors that signal when you are starting to build rapport such, as leaning forward, head tilting, brief eye contact, removing barriers, and mirroring.
- Every culture has nuances in the socially acceptable way to build rapport through greetings, appropriate social distance, use of silence, self-disclosure, and the like. Every culturally agile professional should learn these nuances before working in another country or with someone from another culture.

Keep reading

- Gelb, M. 2017. *The Art of Connection: 7 Relationship-Building Skills Every Leader Needs Now*. Morrisville, NC: New World Library.
- Goleman, D. 2007. *Social Intelligence: The New Science of Human Relationships*. New York: Bantam Books.
- Harley, S. 2013. *How to Say Anything to Anyone: A Guide to Building Business Relationships That Really Work*. Austin, TX: Greenleaf Book Group Press.
- Schafer, J., and Karlins, M. 2015. *The Like Switch: An Ex-FBI Agent's Guide to Influencing, Attracting, and Winning People Over*. New York: Touchstone.

Endnotes

1 Mäkelä, K., and Suutari, V. 2009. "Global Careers: A Social Capital Paradox." *International Journal of Human Resource Management* 20, no. 5: 992–1008.

2 Nielsen, I., Jex, S., and Adams, G. 2000. "Development and Validation of Scores on a Two-Dimensional Workplace Friendship Scale." *Educational and Psychological Measurement* 60, no. 4: 628–643.

3 Caligiuri, P. M. 2000. "Selecting Expatriates for Personality Characteristics: A Moderating Effect of Personality on the Relationship between Host National Contact and Cross-Cultural Adjustment." *Management International Review* 40, no. 1: 61–80.

4 Wilmot, M. P., Wanberg, C. R., Kammeyer-Mueller, J., and Ones, D. S. 2019. "Extraversion Advantages at Work: A Quantitative Review and Synthesis of the Meta-Analytic Evidence." *Journal of Applied Psychology* 104, no. 12: 1447–1470.
5 Furnham, A. 2018. "Dark Side Correlates of Job Reliability and Stress Tolerance in Two Large Samples." *Personality and Individual Differences* 117, no. 15: 255–259.
6 An excellent summary of this research from social psychology is found in Schafer, J., and Karlins, M. 2015. *The Like Switch: An Ex-FBI Agent's Guide to Influencing, Attracting and Winning People Over*. New York: Touchstone.
7 National Association of Colleges and Employers. February 22, 2018. "Employers, Students Differ in Perception of Graduates' 'Career Readiness.'" https://www.naceweb.org/about-us/press/2018/employers-students-differ-in-perception-of-graduates-career-readiness/ (archived at https://perma.cc/38PB-YN3K) [Accessed January 10, 2019].
8 Caligiuri, P., DuBois, C.L.Z., Lundby, K., and Sinclair, E. September 2020. "Fostering International–Domestic Student Integration through an Intervention to Increase Cultural Agility." *Research in Comparative and International Education*, https://doi.org/10.1177/1745499920954311 (archived at https://perma.cc/45LC-KW7D).
9 Bruning, N. S., Sonpar, K., and Wang, X. 2012. "Host-Country National Networks and Expatriate Effectiveness: A Mixed-Methods Study." *Journal of International Business Studies* 43, no. 4: 444–450.
10 Sorokowska, A. et al. 2017. "Preferred Interpersonal Distances: A Global Comparison." *Journal of Cross-Cultural Psychology* 48, no. 4: 577–592.
11 Remland, M., Jones, T., and Brinkman, H. 1995. "Interpersonal Distance, Body Orientation, and Touch: Effects of Culture, Gender, and Age." *Journal of Social Psychology* 135: 281–297.
12 Koudenburg, N., Postmes, T., and Gordijn, E. H. 2011. "Disrupting the Flow: How Brief Silences in Group Conversations Affect Social Needs." *Journal of Experimental Social Psychology* 47, no. 12: 512–515.
13 Trompenaars, A., and Hampden-Turner, C. 2001. *Riding the Waves of Culture: Understanding Diversity in Global Business*, 3rd ed. Boston: Nicholas Brealey Publishing.

07 Perspective taking to empathize and understand people from a different culture

With over twenty years of global experience, Christine Chastain has deep expertise in both design and innovation. As a human-centered innovator, now working as an expert in service design, Christine uses foresight, mixed research methods, and cultural understanding to explore complex questions that lead to the development of strategic design solutions for organizations around the world. "Every question I have been tasked with answering has had me see behaviors and motivations through the eyes of others." Christine believes the responsibility of a designer is to "provide solutions that improve the lives of people being designed for."

Using her expertise in design theory, Christine has led transformational change within organizations using user-centered and strategic design methods. She has been on the founding teams of the Advanced Portfolio Exploration Group at General Motors, the Center for Innovation at Mayo Clinic, and the Innovation Center of Excellence at Cigna. "Whether working on behavioral change or meta change at a policy level, you cannot be successful unless you understand the underlying meaning of the change in those affected," Christine shared. To do this effectively requires a deep appreciation for the cultural context in which the change will be embedded.

Christine has a naturally high level of perspective taking, the ability to put herself in someone else's shoes and imagine how they would react to something. As a culturally agile professional, perspective taking has served her well in a career that has spanned every continent. She sagely shared that perspective taking requires a high level of self-vigilance because you just never know when you slip into a cultural assumption, or cultural bias, always to the detriment of an effort or project.

While working as a creative director on an international assignment in India for Lintas (which was Ammirati Puris Lintas at the time) earlier in her career, Christine, an American, saw the importance of self-vigilance in perspective taking firsthand. Assigned to a team of more than forty to serve clients based primarily in Chennai, Mumbai, and Bangalore on integrated creative solutions, she was the sole foreigner working at the agency in Chennai. There was not much precedent for Christine to follow as a relatively young, foreign female; she needed to rely heavily on her own competencies and instincts.

In the 1990s, at the time of her assignment, India was just starting to open to foreign trade. To make the situation more challenging, Christine's international assignment was based in a relatively traditional and conservative part of India (then Madras, now Chennai). "The India of today barely resembles the India of the 1990s," Christine said.

Every foreign advertising company operating in India brought with them an incredibly talented team of creatives, copywriters, and planners. As a creative director, Christine noted how advertising was a nascent industry and billboards were still drawn by hand on any available surface. From a practical perspective, "trying to match the color and dimensions of a logo in a hand-drawn format was an overt advertising challenge, but there were more subtle cultural challenges that were even more difficult to navigate," she said. Each company needed to navigate the cultural challenges of selling to the Indian consumer while learning to work with their Indian colleagues.

For Christine, some of the greatest cultural challenges were within her team and reflected the rapid change occurring within India. She shared a very salient example about smoking in the office. In the 1990s, countries around the world, including in the United States, were passing laws prohibiting smoking in public places due to the understanding of the dangers of secondhand smoke. As an American, Christine was sensitive to the risk.

In the office, there were two females, both pregnant, and both mentioned to her that they would prefer to work in a smoke-free environment. This seemed straightforward. Everyone in the office was supportive of each other—and happy for their colleagues' growing families; they would, of course, see the importance of creating a smoke-free environment. This seemed like an easy request, or so Christine thought. She crafted a well-constructed memo to the team, requesting that those who smoked walk outside the office door to partake. Included in the memo were risk factors and a solution to address the needs of smokers in the office. Supporting colleagues' healthy pregnancies was noble and clearly acceptable, or so she thought. The memo was sent.

Then, an unexpected thing happened. There was backlash, as smokers continued to smoke in the office as if no memo had gone out. This might have been expected among the smokers, but the nonsmoking men were upset by the memo as well.

The pregnant colleagues felt disrespected but remained quiet, while the other Indian women in the office tried to support their pregnant female colleagues. Suddenly, what began as a small issue became a "woman versus man" conversation as much as a "health advocacy versus habitual convenience" conversation.

Assuming it must be that the smokers were feeling inconvenienced, meetings were called to collectively generate a solution. Christine thought the real issues would surface quickly, but she was wrong. She attended six months of weekly meetings where she repeatedly described the risks of secondhand smoke and balancing solutions to accommodate the smokers.

There was no law to mandate no smoking in offices in 1995. It was not until six years later that a court case in India would recognize that smoking in public was harmful for those breathing the secondhand smoke, prohibiting smoking in public offices. It was another seven years after that initial court case, in 2008, when Indian law prohibited smoking in public places. Christine's memo, which would have been typical in the US in the 1990s, was years ahead of its time in India.

There were more than legal issues at play, as Christine discovered. During the months of discussion and negotiation over the nonsmoking policy facilitated by the general manager, Christine had several "a-ha" moments. They included:

- Indian culture has a long and proud tradition of smoking, dating back to 2000 BC when smoking had medicinal purposes. As a nonsmoking American, Christine had no way of knowing this.
- Christine's memo assumed a US perspective, which was misconstrued as colonial, at worst, or disrespectful and arrogant, at best. Sensitivity to India's colonial past was needed.
- Women in India were in the throes of a feminist movement in the 1990s, particularly at work, and male colleagues were not accustomed to any

pushback from women about their behavior. Being told by a woman "how to behave" produced an immediate negative reaction. Even if the men knew that not smoking in the office was the right change, they were resisting the process of how the change was being made. They dug in.

- The team did not have any experience in communicating on matters of healthy lifestyle choices, so it lacked a framework to guide negotiations.
- Creatives tended to identify with artist, explorer, or outlaw archetypes. In this sense, the self-indulgent smoking behaviors were tolerated under the guise that creatives need to do as they please to be creative.

In hindsight, Christine shared, "I did not read my memo through the eyes of my Indian colleagues." She should have built consensus, working with the most senior (and at that time, male) colleagues first, gaining champions, and allowing influence to work the way it does in hierarchical cultures. In retrospect, Christine added that she "should have learned the history of the culture before predicting the lens through which the situation would be judged." Live and learn.

The lesson from India was a powerful one. Over twenty years later, Christine takes nothing for granted when working across cultures and works hard to gain accuracy on how something will be perceived in the eyes of someone from another culture. This is Christine's perspective taking in action. She understands that the same lens that interprets what we see also filters what we see.

Christine shared that "even a human-centered design approach can be dangerous because it can unwittingly promulgate biases, drive polarization, increase inequity, and skew decision-making." We all need to slow down to understand others' values and experiences by engaging in perspective-taking.

Perspective taking

Perspective taking is the ability to imagine what another person is experiencing with some level of accuracy. At a visual or perceptual level, you might be able to easily imagine how difficult it will be for your vertically limited friend to reach something on a high shelf. Or whether the coffee stain on your shirt will be visible to your colleagues during a meeting. At an emotional or conceptual level, you might actively feel joy or sadness when a friend recounts a happy or sad story. Or when a boorish colleague points out that large coffee stain on your shirt with a glib comment, you might observe your more socially sensitive colleagues cringe. They are empathizing with your embarrassment, feeling how the comment must have been experienced from your perspective. When you laugh off your colleague's rude comment by sharing how, on the way to work, Michelle Obama accidentally spilled her hot coffee on you and that she, feeling badly, autographed a copy of her book, the embarrassment others felt for you quickly changes. Hot coffee (ouch). Michelle Obama (surprise). Autograph (happy).

Both aspects of perspective taking, perceptual and emotional, are fostered as a part of normal childhood development.[1] As social animals, we learn to empathize with others. Those who have difficulty accurately sensing feelings will have a lower level of perspective taking. At an extreme, you have likely heard about this challenge associated with those who have an autism spectrum disorder, people who have greater difficulty in or sometimes an inability to sense the emotions or perceptions of others.[2] At the opposite extreme, those who are considered empaths, about 1 percent of the population, feel others' emotions so deeply that they need to be careful who they "let in" or else they will be crippled by others' feelings. Most people are somewhere in between within the normal range. About 20 percent of the population is on the higher end of normal, the point on the continuum where you will find the best culturally agile professionals.[3]

Perspective taking is a critical cultural agility competency because it enables you to judge situations through a different lens and adapt your behavioral responses, when needed, in cross-cultural situations. In the context of being in a different country or with people from a different culture, perspective taking is the ability to see things from another's point of view, even when their perceptions and emotional responses are different from your own.

Assess your perspective taking

Having an accurate self-awareness of your level of perspective taking is important for your success as a culturally agile professional. This short self-assessment was written as a first step in self-awareness, based on the research on the characteristics present in those who have a high level of perspective taking.

To get a general sense of your perspective taking, read each of the following seven sentences and make an X next to each sentence with which you are in strong agreement. Try not to overthink any question. Usually your first answer is your best one. Choose the response that best describes your attitude or feeling about each statement. Please select the response that comes to mind first when you read the statement.

- ☐ I have been complimented on my ability to work on a creative team, regardless of how diverse the team might be.
- ☐ When someone has a different opinion from mine, I can understand why he or she holds that opinion even if I do not agree.
- ☐ Most people would say I am a good listener. They often will often share things with me because they say I understand them.
- ☐ Compared to most people, I am better at understanding others' perceptions because I ask more questions to ensure I am accurate.
- ☐ When I watch a sad movie, I have deep feelings of sadness (and may even avoid sad movies because I know how they will affect me).
- ☐ Seeing someone upset makes me genuinely upset. It is difficult to remain neutral, especially if the person is a close friend or a loved one.
- ☐ I can accurately sense what others are feeling even if they are not admitting their true feelings.

Count the number of Xs you marked. If you have two or fewer checked, your perspective taking is likely low. If you had five or more checked, your perspective taking is high. And if you are like most people, you had three or four checked and your perspective taking is somewhere in between.

Benefits of perspective taking

Perspective taking might seem like a warm and fuzzy competency, without much place in business. However, having a high level of perspective taking is related to a series of benefits that facilitate the success of culturally agile professionals, helping them gain an accurate understanding of how people, situations, and things are perceived and interpreted. Accuracy is always an advantage in business. Period. People with a higher level of perspective taking become more effective in their technical roles and better leaders of diverse people, teams, and processes.

Have better social connections

As social animals, people feel close to us when we engage in *accurate* perspective taking. Those who engage in perspective taking can only gain that accuracy when they ask questions and actively listen—really listen—to the answer. The best description of active listening is illustrated by the Chinese character "ting," representing listening as an activity requiring our ears, eyes, heart, and undivided attention. The ancient Greek philosopher Epictetus also reminds us that "we have two ears and one mouth so that we can listen twice as much as we speak."

Active listening to engage in perspective taking accurately enables us to show an authentic interest in the other person, which is central for relationship formation. When someone listens and seeks to understand our perspective, we feel "heard." This, quite naturally, makes us feel more connected to the other person. As Maya Angelou once said, "I've learned that people will forget what you said, people will forget what you did, but people will never forget how you made them feel." Social connections form. As a tie that binds, the power of active listening is universal.

Be more accurate in how others see a situation

It is a natural human tendency to interpret new situations in a way that fits our expectations and simultaneously ignores deviations from what we expect. The same lens that interprets what we see also filters what we see, which can reduce our accuracy in perspective taking. The reason for this is a natural human tendency to observe that which fits our expectations and simultaneously ignore deviations from what we expect to see. This is called the confirmation bias—and it is as human as breathing. We have a hard time seeing things we are not expecting. As a great visual, you might remember seeing the video of the "moonwalking bear." (If you have not seen the video, look for it on YouTube.)

When we engage in perspective taking, we become more conscious of our default interpretation of a situation and have a heightened ability to imagine plausible alternative perceptions of the same situation. Research has found that bilingual individuals are particularly good at this because they have honed their cognitive flexibility whereby multiple words can be used to describe the same thing. Your perspective taking works the same way. It begins with an ability to provide multiple explanations for the same observation.

Your perspective taking also stops you from making reflexive judgments. You pause long enough to not trust your initial belief of what someone should be perceiving or feeling. This pause gives your brain a chance to develop plausible alternative explanations and then, through that active listening, to determine which is the accurate explanation given the cross-cultural context.

Increase accuracy in how others see you

With a higher level of perspective taking, you will not only understand situations from another lens, but you will also be able to see yourself and your behaviors from another cultural perspective. In doing so, you will be able to anticipate how your behaviors, communication style, gestures, and even emails might be interpreted through another set of eyes. For example, if you were raised as a child to refer to adults by their first name and, as an adult, you work for a company where everyone is on a first-name basis regardless of level, then you have probably been socialized in an egalitarian and informal culture. As a culturally agile professional, when working in a more formal culture, you can sense how your informality could be viewed negatively and, in turn, adjust to a more formal style to show respect, gain credibility, and build trust. In other words, you can see how behavior appropriate in your own culture, such as using a senior leader's first name or wearing jeans to work, could be viewed as inappropriate in the culture where you are working.

Cultural challenges in perspective taking

Even people with the highest level of perspective taking in a domestic context can be ineffective in a cross-cultural context because their empathy, necessary for perspective taking, is diluted in an unfamiliar cross-cultural setting. Your empathy emerges when you successfully read facial cues, register tone of voice, and interpret gestures and posture.[4] Most of these visual and auditory cues, however, have different meanings depending on the culture in which we were socialized. For example, closing one's eyes during a meeting might indicate boredom or napping, unless you are in Japan, where it might mean that someone is concentrating. Then again, it could also mean that your Japanese colleague is sleepy, making this difficult to discern unless you are familiar with the Japanese culture.

Research has found that our empathic accuracy is at its highest when we are with people who are demographically similar (e.g., same age, profession, sex, race, nationality). From a cultural perspective, research has found that we are more accurate in predicting emotional responses when the other person is from our same culture. In one study, when people were shown photos of culturally similar and culturally diverse individuals in positive situations (e.g., smiling at a party) and negative situations (e.g., experiencing grief), they were able to accurately interpret positive and negative emotions for those who were from the same culture.[5] It was more difficult when people were from another culture.

Even when other situational cues exist, it is challenging to be accurate when interpreting people and predicting situational responses across cultures. Perspective taking across cultures is a skill, a practiced art. It can be learned if you engage in two things: *finding similarity* and *interpreting perceptual differences.*

Find similarity

In addition to demographic similarity, experiential similarity also produces a greater empathic response because we have a greater empathic connection with those with whom we have a shared life experience (e.g., being in the military, playing the same sport, having an elderly parent who is ill). An important skill for all culturally agile professionals is learning how to (quickly) find similarity with people from different cultures, whether it is a shared interest in cricket, a shared birth year, or a love for spicy food. Finding such similarities gives your perspective taking a metaphorical caffeine boost in another cultural context.

Finding similarity is a skill that can be fostered with a bit of practice. In one study, my colleagues and I had culturally diverse dyads (one person from one culture and another person from a different culture) meet five times over the course of ten weeks and, in each meeting, structure their conversations around what they have in common.[6] My favorite reported similarity was two undergraduate students, one from China and one from the United States, who both dressed as Harry Potter when they were eleven years old. At the end of the ten-week study, participants' openness toward people from other cultures was increased. I have repeated this activity in many corporate and university settings, always with great success.

I am certain you have heard a less contrived version of this study countless times listening to conversations of people who do not know each other well. *Oh, really, you are the youngest of five? So am I. You lived in Buffalo, New York? I did too. Wow. We have a lot in common.* For many people, the more they engage in finding similarities with people from different cultures, the more their perspective taking competency will build.

Interpret perceptual differences

Once someone from a different culture is brought into your metaphorical in-group, whether because of a Harry Potter costume or a shared commiseration over raising teenagers, you are more likely to want to understand their perspective on other issues. The caution in a cross-cultural context is to assume that a shared similarity on one topic gives you an ability to accurately interpret another person's behaviors or perceptions. This is a myth of similarity that lulls us into believing we can read cross-cultural cues accurately. I promise you that reading such clues is far more difficult than it seems, even for the most seasoned global professionals.

We gain accuracy from shared experiences and values that are socialized from our generation, education, religion, profession, and the like. It is the reason close-knit family members and close friends can sense when something is wrong with one of their loved ones. The more socializing agents you share, the higher the accuracy of perspective taking.

Once you have given your brain license to empathize or engage in perspective taking with another person because of some perceived similarity, the next goal is to interpret perceptual differences accurately.[7] To do this, you will need to actively slow down your cognitive processing. This might sound odd, but it is a valuable piece of advice, given how our brains work.

With colleagues from your own culture, you can intuitively process facial expressions, gestures, and situational cues. Especially with close colleagues you know well, you can rely on the split-second emotional responses of your brain's limbic system and have a better chance at being accurate than you would in another cultural context.[8]

When working in another culture, you will need to process more deliberately using your prefrontal cortex to slow the response and engage in respectful inquiry to generate what might be perceived. In other words, do not assume. Ask. Conscious processing of cross-cultural situations and behaviors will give you a chance to formulate alternatives without rushing to judgment. Your brain will want you to react quickly—both emotionally and intuitively. You need to ignore the immediate reaction and suspend judgment until you better understand the cultural context.

Once you have built your brain's memory bank with plausible alternative cultural interpretations, your accuracy and processing will speed up again. Cross-cultural perspective taking is like learning to drive a car in a country which drives on the opposite side of the road. Over time and with practice, driving on either side of the road can become cognitively effortless. Until then, slow down.

Cultural differences in the expression of perspective taking

While the skill of active listening, fundamental for perspective taking, is universal, the way we ask questions and receive answers is not. Discussing every nuance of cross-cultural communication would be beyond the scope of this book, but a few are particularly important when you engage in perspective taking across cultures.

Differences in privacy and self-disclosure

Culturally agile professionals need to respect the cross-cultural differences in privacy and self-disclosure. Cultures differ in the extent to which they seem open, approachable, or accessible when asking questions about feelings or perceptions. If you asked your colleagues, "What did you think of the keynote speaker?," you might get a detailed critique from some colleagues and a short "fine" from others, who might prefer a private conversation to share their feedback. Proceed with caution when asking questions in a cross-cultural context, beginning with neutral questions to determine how comfortable the individual is with sharing feelings and perceptions. Ask those questions in a private conversation to remove the cross-cultural differences in proffering opinions in public.

When seeking to find a connection to establish empathy, keep in mind that cultures differ in terms of how long it takes to disclose personal information. In some cultural contexts, you should maintain an emotional distance and not ask personal questions until trust is established. In these cultures, it would seem intrusive to ask about topics such as health, a family member's health, a child's education, and the like. In other cultural contexts, sharing personal information is the way to expedite the formation of trust. Those exact same topics would evoke a sense of caring and empathy. When in doubt, ask someone in your network (who understands the culture well) to guide you on the social norms for self-disclosure and privacy.

Differences in who is trusted

In relationship-oriented cultures, such as many parts of Asia, Africa, and South America, trust—a willingness to share information—will come only after time has been invested to foster solid professional relationships. In relationship-oriented cultures, you are advised to use an intermediary or consultant to help facilitate interviews, conversations, and immersion experiences. In task-oriented cultures, such as many countries in northern Europe and North America, professional trust is formed through the effectiveness of the person in the role.

Differences in giving direct answers

Direct cultures are low-context communicators (Americans, Germans, and the Dutch to name a few). Professionals from these cultures often are perplexed by how little they really understand when working in higher-context cultures. High-context communication is indirect; therefore, the true meaning of words cannot be readily interpreted without fully understanding other subtle cues. These cues are often invisible to (or misinterpreted by) those who have not lived in the culture long enough to understand them. In high-context cultures, you will need to work with cultural insiders to gather accurate information.

Differences in hierarchy

Ideas that are shared or by the senior person in the room might be weighed more heavily. In hierarchical cultures, such as China or India, team members might be unwilling to express their opinions or true feelings in the presence of a senior leader who will either speak first (to project the outcome) or last (to synthesize the outcome). In egalitarian cultures, such as Sweden or Denmark, ideas and opinions would be more comfortably expressed by any colleague, regardless of level.

The role of the group

Instead of interpretations being understood through the lens of one person, as would occur in countries like the US and Canada, understanding perspectives might require that the group be allowed to form a collective perception that is conveyed by the group so no one person is responsible for any given perception or feeling. In collectivist cultures through Asia, Africa, South America, and the Middle East, you will often hear individuals use the phrase "We believe..." or "We think..." To gain accuracy, in collectivist cultures you might want to give colleagues enough time to prepare their group-level response.

Build your perspective taking

You can build your perspective taking by practicing the behaviors of slowing interpretations, forming alternative interpretations, and active listening. Here are some suggestions for behavioral changes you can start today to build your capacity for perspective taking.

Form alternative explanations as a creative process

When you make an observation, your initial perception is the one that directly corresponds with your greatest store of memories—the mental data you have gathered over the years to explain social behavior. Your memories form the foundation for your intuition and judgment about people. If you are like many, your store of memories has been created within one country or with one cultural lens. You can learn how to form alternative explanations as a creative process, the ability to look at a situation and try to come up with as many possible interpretations as possible. Give this a try the next time you have the chance to inconspicuously observe people (e.g., waiting in line, at a park). If there are people talking, observe their interactions and try to imagine all of the possible ways they might know each other. If they are walking, observe their expressions and try to imagine all of the possible places they might be going. Remember, this is a creative process.

Think like an anthropologist

With people you know well, practice tracing their observable behaviors back to the socializing agents that have influenced those attitudes, values, and beliefs. Socializing agents can be family, schools attended, professional affiliations, past employers, and the country in which they live—just to name a few. Do the same analysis for yourself. Remember that neither you nor anyone else was born with their norms, values, or assumptions. Each person was socialized at some point in life. Knowing someone's nationality is not the same as understanding their values and assumptions; nationality is only one socializing agent—but one in which others, such as education and family, are embedded. To better predict another person's perceptions and feelings, you will need to understand deeply how they have been socialized.

Understand the similarity effect in perspective taking

The next time you are in a public place and have a minute or two to spare, try this exercise: First, focus on your own emotional state. Are you tired? Ready for lunch? Happy? Worried about a family member? Whatever the state is, really focus on it. Then scan around the room to find someone who is most like you from the perspective of demography: about the same age, same sex, same ethnicity, and so on. Try to imagine that he or she is feeling the exact same emotions as you. Really give yourself a minute to imagine this. (Doing this should be relatively easy.) Repeat this exercise one more time. This time find someone demographically different from you—different age, opposite sex, and so on. Try to imagine the person is feeling the exact same emotions as you are feeling. Give yourself a minute to sense their emotions. If you are like most people, the latter exercise will be more challenging than the former. This exercise is a good reminder that it is easier to empathize with people we perceive to be similar to ourselves.

Debate yourself to practice forming alternate opinions

If you have a strong political affiliation, religious belief, or social cause for which you feel passionate, try to imagine the validity of the opposite extreme. Debate with yourself around some key issues, accepting the plausibility of the opposite extreme. If it is just too difficult to imagine an alternate opinion around an issue for which you feel strongly, try to imagine an objective third-party individual. Think through how that person could potentially view both your side and the other as concurrently valid. You do not need to agree with the alternative perspective, just acknowledge it as valid from a different lens.

Ask questions to test your assumptions

Practice differentiating between what you observe in others—facts—from what you infer they are sensing or feeling from their behaviors—the hypotheses or assumptions you make. Work to clarify hypotheses and assumptions in your daily life; it is a habit that will serve you well in situations when "getting to the facts" might be more challenging. When possible, check your assumptions with those about whom the assumptions are being made—or with credible cultural resources who can interpret behavior more accurately.

Key takeaways

- Perspective taking is the ability to *accurately* understand how someone from a different culture is seeing things.
- To kickstart perspective taking, try to find similarity with those from a different culture. Similarity will foster your natural desire to empathize.
- Do not assume you can accurately interpret what others are feeling or perceiving. You will need more knowledge of the cultural context to foster accuracy.
- Perspective taking enables you to form better social connections, gain accuracy in perceptions, and know how you appear across cultures.
- Some dimensions of perspective taking have a cultural component that will influence how you engage in this competency.
- Perspective taking is a skill, a practiced act. You can build this skill by practicing the behaviors of slowing interpretations, forming alternative interpretations, and active listening.

Keep reading

- Gladwell, M. 2019. *Talking to Strangers: What We Should Know about the People We Don't Know*. Boston: Little, Brown and Company.
- Riess, H. 2018. *The Empathy Effect: Seven Neuroscience-Based Keys for Transforming the Way We Live, Love, Work, and Connect across Differences*. Boulder, CO: Sounds True.
- Zaki, J. 2019. *The War for Kindness: Building Empathy in a Fractured World*. New York: Crown.

Endnotes

1 Marvin, R. S., Greenberg, M. T., and Mossler, D. G. 1976. "The Early Development of Conceptual Perspective Taking: Distinguishing among Multiple Perspectives Child Development." *Child Development* 47, no. 2: 511–514.

2 Roeyers, H., Buysse, A., Ponnet, K., and Pichal, B. 2001. "Advancing Advanced Mind-Reading Tests: Empathic Accuracy in Adults with a Pervasive Developmental Disorder." *Journal of Child Psychology and Psychiatry* 42, no. 2: 271–278.

3 Acevedo, B. P., Aron, E. N., Aron, A., Sangster, M. D., Collins, N., and Brown, L. L. 2014. "The Highly Sensitive Brain: An fMRI Study of Sensory Processing Sensitivity and Response to Others' Emotions." *Brain Behavior* 4: 580–594.

4 Reiss, H. 2018. *The Empathy Effect*. Boulder, CO: Sounds True.

5 Neumann D. L., Boyle G. J., and Chan R.C.K. 2013. "Empathy towards Individuals of the Same and Different Ethnicity When Depicted in Negative and Positive Contexts." *Personality and Individual Differences* 55, no. 1: 8–13.

6 Caligiuri, P., DuBois, C.L.Z., Lundby, K., and Sinclair, E. September 2020. "Fostering International–Domestic Student Integration through an Intervention to Increase Cultural Agility." *Research in Comparative and International Education*, 15, no. 4: 357–370.

7 Hodges, S. D., Kiel, K. J., Kramer, A.D.I., Veach, D., and Villanueva, B. R. 2010. "Giving Birth to Empathy: The Effects of Similar Experience on Empathic Accuracy, Empathic Concern, and Perceived Empathy." *Personality and Social Psychology Bulletin* 36, no. 3: 398–409.

8 Stinson, L., and Ickes, W. 1992. "Empathic Accuracy in the Interactions of Male Friends versus Male Strangers." *Journal of Personality and Social Psychology* 62, no. 5: 787–797.

PART THREE
Task-management competencies

Kimberly Jung is a social entrepreneur and former military officer (Captain, US Army) with a Harvard MBA and a master's degree in engineering from MIT. Kim was born in Chinatown in Los Angeles to immigrant parents from Hong Kong. Both of Kim's parents realized the American dream quickly, her father as a chemical engineer and politician and her mother as a real estate controller for the county.

From the familiarity of Chinatown, Kim's parents raised her to be extraordinary, to focus on academic and career success and lock in on her goals and achieve them. From an early age, she played piano competitively, started studying for the SATs by seventh grade, and volunteered at local soup kitchens. I was my "Asian tiger mom's dream," Kim said. Her parents taught her to "appreciate every opportunity, sit in the front, disregard silly societal norms, pick yourself up when you fall, pick others up, save money constantly, finish all the food on your plate, and believe in your own abilities, capacity to learn, and robustness to survive anything." Kim was taught to envision goals and use hard work, creativity, and optimism to realize them.

Kim took her parents' advice to a level they never imagined, locking in on goals and defying every possible cultural norm of a California girl from Chinatown. Culture was context for Kim, not prescription or destiny. As a Southern California teenager, most (including her parents) would have predicted that Kim would attend Stanford and play beach volleyball. Instead, she went to West Point, graduating in 2008 with a bachelor's degree in mechanical engineering. Her goal as a seventeen-year-old was "to see the world, lead soldiers into battle, prove my athletic ability, and serve my country." The army enabled her to achieve these goals, stationed in Germany and later serving in Afghanistan.

While serving a deployment in Afghanistan in 2010 and 2011, Kim was an engineer officer and platoon leader with RCP 44, 2nd Platoon, 535 ESC. Her platoon removed roadside bombs and faced ambushes along craggy roads in remote villages. Successful in her missions, Kim used cultural agility to gain the trust of host nationals by drinking tea with elders and spending time with Afghan village women, listening to their hopes and dreams. She reflects on her experiences with Afghan villagers as a time when she experienced the greatest sense of fulfillment, humanity, and humility.

To solve challenges that seemed culturally insurmountable in these villages, she encouraged her platoon to keep an open mind and engage with locals and learn from them. Kim and a couple of her squad leaders went to the Afghan National Army base across the street and invited the Afghan troops to engage in joint missions together. The initiative was not born out of any orders from a higher commander but from creativity and improvisation in the face of uncertainty. Kim's platoon was alone in a remote area, far from headquarters and maintenance support. They needed to figure out a way to make allies locally, which meant engaging enthusiastically with local key players. Culture was the context to be understood and to be worked around for Kim but not the deterrent from the broader goal. Kim practiced cultural agility as she locked in on goals and creatively developed solutions that might be considered counterculture.

On one of these missions, the Afghan platoon brought dried legs of meat to their American counterparts. The American soldiers in her platoon were skeptical of the food and the motivation behind the offering. On the contrary, Kim quickly recognized this as a symbol of solidarity, that sharing a meal was an important way to build relationships in the Afghan culture. Quieting the grumbles of her soldiers, Kim and her squad leaders overtly pronounced deep gratitude to their Afghan counterparts and urged the platoon to graciously accept the gift, share the meal, and thank the Afghan soldiers. In turn, the American soldiers shared their MREs (meal ready-to-eat) and bottled water, a reciprocal gesture the Afghan soldiers graciously accepted.

With this Afghan platoon, the trusting relationship could flourish because some of the platoon leaders were welcoming to Kim. Others were not as friendly. Some Afghan platoon leaders refused to even acknowledge Kim's presence because she was a woman, even though she was the American platoon leader. Kim, using her cultural agility, recognized that this was not the moment to assert her rank, as doing so would not be helpful to foster trusting relationships. Kim encouraged her platoon sergeant, a man who reported to her, to take the lead in the conversation with those Afghan military leaders. The mission was successful. With this cultural backdrop, Kim left Afghanistan with a special place in her heart for the plight of Afghan women.

Kim's ability to understand culture as the context in which goals would be achieved brought her back to Afghanistan in 2013, this time as a social entrepreneur. In 2013, while Kim was attending Harvard Business School, she fondly remembered the Afghan women and farmers she had met during her deployment. Motivated by her entrepreneurship professor, Shikhar Ghosh, she locked in a new goal to create a small business which could contribute to a sustainable foundation for peace in Afghanistan.

As a foodie, Kim knew that Afghan farmers grew the most amazing saffron in the world. Their limitation was that they could not break through to the global market with their current level of packaging, marketing, quality, and sanitation. With the idea for a company, Kim returned to Afghanistan, now as a civilian, to meet with local farmers over tea and mangoes. Speaking through interpreters to traditional farmers who were unwilling to shake hands (as doing so would have been culturally inappropriate), she knew the farmers would be suspicious of her motives. Nonetheless, like her experience as a female military leader in Afghanistan, Kim saw the cultural challenges as merely the context to be understood; her goal was to start a sustainable business in Afghanistan. Kim locked in on the goal.

The moment she saw that most spectacular saffron packaged in a dusty cardboard box wrapped in string, Kim's vision for Rumi Spice was set; working around the cultural challenges just added to the thrill.

From Rumi Spice's webpage:

> Named after the Persian poet Jalal al-Din Rumi, our company partners with Afghan farmers to bring top-quality, sustainably farmed saffron to the international market. Started by a team of US military veterans who served combat tours in Afghanistan, Rumi sources saffron from local Afghan farms and employs more than 3,750 women in Herat, Afghanistan to hand-harvest the delicate stigmas of the flowers. Committed to empowering Afghan women and bolstering the country's economy, Rumi reinvests back into agricultural

> and manufacturing infrastructure. In Afghanistan, we have stood up three processing facilities with over 300 farmers in our network. We make up 3.6% of Afghanistan's total foreign direct investment in agriculture. We are laying a foundation for peace, one saffron flower at a time.

The steps to get from the vision to the success of Rumi Spice were not easy, given the many cultural challenges. In Afghanistan, for example, it is expected that everyone sits on a carpeted floor as they process and package the saffron. From a hygiene perspective, Kim knew that this was a practice that would negatively affect quality and purity standards. She needed to create a sterile environment with chairs and workstations.

It took two years to change the norms. In those years, Kim remained firm about not having carpets and instituting handwashing and mask wearing. Workers were hired according to their abilities to abide by these norms, and local national quality managers were brought on to continually reinforce the norms. The behaviors, while not consistent with the Afghan culture, were nonnegotiable for working at Rumi Spice. To motivate these behaviors, Kim underscored how, without them, there would be no business and no income. She explained to the workers that the Whole Foods buyers, the American Food and Drug Administration, and health inspectors would never stand for carpeted floors in a facility. The more the workers trusted Kim as a leader with their best interests at heart, the more they willingly adapted their behaviors.

Kim won the workers' respect by demonstrating her commitment to them and was consistently a person of her word. Today, Rumi Spice reaches the highest Category I in the International Standards Organization for saffron quality. "You can shift cultural norms if you do so in a respectful and humble way," said Kim. The women who work at Rumi Spice now wear uniforms and work in a sterile environment appropriate for food production. The farmers now shake Kim's hand, seeing her first as their American partner and not as a woman. Having shared goals help shift cultural norms; they are the context and not the destiny.

Kim has the right to be proud of Rumi Spice as the company's spices are sought out by chefs from the finest restaurants in the United States. Rumi Spice employees thousands of women who are paid directly, and the farmers' families have more than tripled their incomes.

Kim added, "I am proud that the company I cofounded is making progress towards a better future for Afghanistan, for farmers, for women, one saffron flower at a time."

Like Kim, as a culturally agile professional, you will need to understand the demands of the cross-cultural context and respond effectively within it. In my research, I have found that every culturally agile professional has three of these responses, which I call task-management competencies. They are like tools in your toolbox:

- **Cultural adaptation** is the ability to successfully change your behaviors to match the behavioral norms of the cross-cultural context. In this response, you are doing it *their way*. In Kim's case, she used cultural adaptation when working with male Afghan military leaders who did not want to speak with her as a woman, irrespective of her high rank. Given the goal of the mission, Kim adapted her behaviors and allowed her more junior male colleagues to interact with the Afghans.
- **Cultural minimization** is the ability to uphold standards even when doing so might mean instituting something that is counter to cultural norms. In this response, they are doing it *your way*. Kim used cultural minimization to enable Rumi Spice to succeed in the global economy with tighter standards for quality and purity. Even though uniforms, workstations, and a sterile environment were not consistent with Afghan norms, Kim was able to accomplish the goal.
- **Cultural integration** is the ability to create an entirely new set of cultural norms within a group where no single cultural norm is dominant. In this response, you and they are creating *a new way*. Kim used cultural integration as she helped to foster the organizational culture of Rumi Spice. Walking into the company, it does not appear as either an American or an Afghan company. Rather, the culture of the company that emerged is uniquely its own.

Deciding which of these three tools—adaptation, minimization, or integration—to pull out of the toolbox is contingent on the context and the demands of the situation. For culturally agile professionals, one tool is neither better nor worse. Each tool has different uses for different situations. Many professionals working cross-culturally run into problems when they use the wrong response. They are trying to use the wrong tool for the job, so to speak. This will resonate with anyone who has tried to hammer a nail with a screwdriver and made a mess of the wall. (Maybe that was just me.) Either way, we need to discuss all three responses as unique abilities, but, it is worth repeating, there is no one higher-order response. You will need to use the right response given the goal of the cross-cultural situation.

Each of these three task management competencies—adaptation, minimization, and integration—is a specific cultural response which requires a unique set of skills. The skills for cultural adaptation are discussed in Chapter 8. The skills for cultural minimization are covered in Chapter 9, and cultural integration's skills are covered in Chapter 10.

Cultural adaptation to respond as expected in a culturally diverse situation 08

Cultural adaptation is the ability to successfully change your behaviors to match the norms of the cross-cultural context. When using this response, you are behaving like others are expecting you to behave. This is often thought of as the "when in Rome" approach.

An academic friend and coauthor, Professor Jaime Bonache, pointed out that the origins of the "when in Rome" adage can be traced back 1,600 years.[1] He shared that in the fourth century, various Christian cities differed in how they adhered to religious practices. Saint Augustine's mother, who traveled with Augustine, was upset to learn how Milan's religious practices differed and needed guidance on the best way to be an observant Christian. Augustine, unsure of how to respond to his mother, asked Saint Ambrose, the Bishop of Milan at the time, for advice. Augustine described the advice Ambrose offered in this way:

> When my mother followed me to Milan, she found the Church there was not fasting on Saturday. She began to be troubled, and to hesitate as to what she should do; upon which I, though not taking a personal interest then in such things, applied on her behalf to Ambrose, of most blessed memory, for his advice. He answered that he could not teach me anything but what he himself practiced, because if he knew any better rule, he would observe it himself... And said:

> "When I visit Rome, I fast on Saturday; when I am here, I do not fast. On the same principle, observe the custom prevailing in whatever Church you come to, if you desire neither to give offence by your conduct, nor to find cause of offence in another's." When I reported this to my mother, she accepted it gladly.[2]

Saint Ambrose's advice to his mother is the first recorded use of "When in Rome, do as the Romans do." While enduring, the role of the adage in our lives has changed slightly in over 1,600 years. Today, the line is often used to give ourselves mental permission to do something in a novel context that we would not ordinarily do. A few examples:

- When offered another glass of grappa after a dinner with colleagues in Rome, Kevin responded "When in Rome" before accepting more of the strong liquor. Kevin generally does not drink much, especially during the workweek.
- The bus Janine was waiting for in Mumbai appeared to be tilting perilously in one direction, due to overcrowding. While boardings she muttered "When in Rome" as she was pushed up against strangers.
- Carlos was invited to sing karaoke while in Tokyo with clients. Trying to impress the group, he thought "When in Rome" before giving an off-key performance of "You've Lost That Loving Feeling" to the delight of his clients.
- Asif was invited to join Finnish colleagues for a (naked) sauna. As a normally modest guy, he responded "When in Rome" as he followed his colleagues into the sauna wearing only his birthday suit.

These "when in Rome" situations share one feature: Someone is behaving in a way he or she would not behave at home because the behaviors would be considered unwise, embarrassing, or a reason for possible arrest. In these more extreme situations of adaptation, "when in Rome" provides the response to close the cognitive dissonance and quiet our brain's admonishing tone. While most professional situations requiring cultural adaptation will be far more subtle than a naked sauna, they can, nonetheless, cause you an equal level of discomfort because of the dissonance created between how you are behaving and what those behaviors mean to you.

Consider the example of Anna. Anna started a new job with a relatively small company in the tech industry. During orientation at a table in a room nicknamed the "playroom" (for all the Nerf toys, pinball machines, Ping-Pong and air hockey tables), Anna was advised that the organizational culture was relaxed, light-hearted, and casual—a statement obvious to anyone not both visually and hearing impaired. The conversations were loud, fast-paced, brief, and expressive. The office décor was dorm room chic. The dress code was "who cares about fashion" casual. To fit in, she knew she would need to change her formal style, one honed from years working in her past two roles at conservative financial services firms.

Thinking it would be easy to be in such a relaxed environment, Anna was surprised at the dissonance this informality created for her. Her natural preference for formality gave her a nagging "something is wrong" feeling when she was presenting important content with funny memes and wearing jeans. That feeling was Anna's brain signaling to her that she was acting unprofessionally in a professional context.

When she first started, Anna wore her suits and reverted to a more formal style for presentations, convincing herself that this would show her respect for the organization and underscore the gravitas of her recommendations. The opposite happened; her message was lost because her formality signaled subconsciously that the recommendations she offered were "wrong" for the company.

It only took a few of these negative experiences, ones where her colleagues did not buy into her recommendations, for Anna to fully grasp the importance of adapting to the employer's informal organizational culture. She understood that, as the messenger, her formal style was distracting from the message. "It was not about me. It was about the work. When in Rome, after all," she added.

Over time Anna felt more comfortable in the casual style and even started appreciating the professional benefits of a more open organizational culture. Problems surfaced and could be addressed quickly because lines of communication were not clogged by formality and hierarchy. Anna adapted to the new culture.

While Anna never left her home country, she needed to use cultural adaptation to be effective in the new organizational culture. She needed her cultural agility.

Cultural adaptation, in any new context, will require you to (1) understand the situations in which adaptation is likely needed and (2) learn the process for effectively changing your behaviors and approaches to fit the unfamiliar context.

Situations requiring cultural adaptation

There is a wide variety of tasks, roles, situations, and jobs in which cultural adaptation is needed. Identifying when this approach is needed usually can be accomplished with these four questions:

- *Is there a company policy, industry regulation, or national law to which you must adapt?* You would be breaking the law or unable to conduct business if you did not adapt. Adaptation in this case is nonnegotiable.
- *Are you selling (versus buying)?* Selling is any situation where you need to persuade or influence another person to buy into your idea, approach, product, or service. Adaptation is strongly advised for a better subjective perception of your professional attributes such as trustworthiness, credibility, competence, warmth, and the like. Adaptation in this situation is recommended.
- *Are you leading?* If someone is to follow you, they need to first believe you are trustworthy—credible and worthy of respect. The behaviors you exhibit will affect the way you are perceived, and you might need to adapt these behaviors based on the cultural context.
- *Is there a work outcome that is set without a structured protocol for how the outcome is achieved?* This question is broad and will force you to work back from the desired goal to determine how to best achieve the goal in the cultural context.

Adhering to policies, regulations, and laws

In some situations, your cultural adaptation will be nonnegotiable. Think of how you drive. You would not drive on the left side of the road in the United States or the right side of the road in the United Kingdom. Both would violate traffic laws and would be hazardous to your (and everyone's else's) safety. In a professional context, you might need some form of certification, credential, or license before starting to work. Likewise, there might be standards or regulations governing your industry or profession in that cultural context, controlled through inspections, audits, reports, evaluations, and the like. There might also be country-level institutions, such as laws and unions, affecting how you can accomplish your work in each country. All of these require cultural adaptation. All are nonnegotiable.

Selling

When I refer to "selling" in this case, I am talking about any situation where you will need trust to persuade, negotiate, and strengthen relationships. Perceptions of trust are culturally determined, meaning there are socialized expectations for how trustworthy people will act. The more you adhere to the expected behaviors in context, the more you will be considered trustworthy.[3] In Anna's case, her recommendations were not "sold" because her formal style did not inspire trust among her informal colleagues. If you are the one selling the idea, concept, plan, product, or service, then adapt to the expectations of the context you are in. In this context, you will do yourself a favor and make your life easier by working with (not against) the subconscious processors (i.e., brains) of others.

Cultural adaptation is especially true for client development, marketing, customer service, and most situations in which colleagues, customers, and clients do not know you. In a series of studies, Chanthika Pornpitakpan examined how Japanese, Thai, Chinese, Malaysian, and Indonesian buyers responded to various level of cultural adaptation by American sellers.[4] The more the Americans were perceived to adapt their manners, greetings, dress, and the like, the higher their perceived trustworthiness. For example, Thai clients perceived the American sales team more positively and were anticipating a better sales outcome when the Americans dressed in Thai suits, accepted invitations to lunch with the Thais to build rapport, used the proper Thai form of addressing them by name, and used more subtle gestures. Similarly, the Japanese clients thought more favorably of the American sales team and also anticipated a better sales outcome when the Americans used the Japanese way of exchanging business cards, invested time in the relationship before discussing business, and addressed them with the proper Japanese title.

There is a caveat to this rule of thumb to "adapt when selling": situations when your natural style represents an ideal or preferred state. In these cases, your appearance, communication, and behaviors will trigger positive perceptions of trust because they represent an aspirational ideal and fit the image of what one is expecting. For example, if you are a furniture or clothing designer, appearing more creative in front of prospective retail customers could have the intended (and positive) cognitive trigger. Your creative aura triggers the perception of being cutting edge. If you are in private equity, your flawless style might inspire tremendous confidence for a client organization with a less professional style. You polished style provides the association of financial success. In these cases, you have an intentional reason to want to be perceived in a different, possibly countercultural, way. My experience is that deviating from expected norms when selling needs to be used carefully.

Leading

If you are in a leadership role, the goals for your team might appear to have little need for cultural adaptation. However, the behaviors involved in being perceived (and followed) as a leader will often need to be adapted. For example, while operating in more egalitarian cultures, such as the Nordic countries, Australia, and Canada, you might be best advised to encourage employees to call you by your first name, regardless of title, education, or level in the company. In these cultures, there is a belief that people from any background or any start point can rise to power. You are no different and are not afforded more respect solely because of your rank. This sense of equality gives everyone—from highest to lowest in the organization—an equal voice. In this context you might need to adapt to being confronted openly and to not expect power and authority to be given to you just because you have a title. You will need to adapt to earn respect and be a great team builder.

The opposite might be true if you are leading people who have been socialized in Asia, the Middle East, Africa, southern Europe, and South America. In these cultures, there is often a preference for hierarchy. With employees from these cultures, be ready to provide clear direction, have executive presence, and have the answers when you are asked questions. The bottom line is that you will need to behave as the leader that your followers want to follow.

Organizing how work is accomplished

Compared to the previous situations warranting cultural adaptation, organizing how work is accomplished has no easy rules to follow. This form of cultural adaptation occurs when you know *what* your work outcome should be but have full latitude in determining *how* the work should be accomplished. In some cases, the best approach is to use cultural adaptation; in others, it will be one of the other two cultural responses, cultural minimization (Chapter 9) or cultural integration (Chapter 10).

Consider the case of American workers who worked both abroad and in the United States under the same job title of public relations, economic analyst, and political analyst. Research found that while the tangible outcomes did not change as a function of working in another country, the way in which they performed their jobs did based on culture.[5] When they were in more group-oriented countries, they leveraged relationship-oriented, responses including coordinating, developing, and building teams. In individual-oriented cultures, they operated independently. The team-oriented and coordination tasks were performed less frequently. The same job with the same goals was accomplished in different ways depending on the culture.

Sometimes you will need to adapt how you organize the work of others. Consider the manufacturing goal of productivity. Researcher Giles Hirst and his colleagues compared the productivity of manufacturing facilities in the United Kingdom and China.[6] In both cases, the workers were encouraged to have greater autonomy (e.g., greater discretion to make decisions and control over their work). This method of working was welcome in the United Kingdom, where the production workers felt less stress with higher autonomy. The opposite was true in China, where the Chinese production workers felt more stressed. While stress negatively affected outcomes in both cases, mitigating the stress with autonomy was a good idea in only one culture.

The focus for determining whether to adapt how work should be accomplished depends on the tangible outcomes and whether a culturally consistent approach would be best to achieve those outcomes. Every situation needs to be evaluated independently.

Skills of cultural adaptation

Through my consulting and teaching at the university, I have had the privilege to work with thousands of people who need to effectively leverage the cultural response of adaptation. Some are students studying abroad in an educational system with a different set of behavioral norms for academic achievement, classroom protocol, interactions with faculty, and the like. These students need to adapt their behaviors to succeed in their academic programs. Some are employees who need to work collaboratively on a multicultural team where the dominant norm is different from their own. They need to adapt to fit into the team culture. Some are professionals who need to adapt their behaviors to build trust, gain credibility, and successfully influence to ensure a positive outcome.

Whether a nineteen-year-old student or a sixty-nine-year-old executive, you will need to master two things to effectively use cultural adaptation:

1 You will need to *learn the new behaviors*. By competently mastering the new behaviors, you will be perceived as "blending in" because you are

behaving in a way that is consistent with others' expectations. You might not be a natural at those behaviors, but you are neither cringeworthy nor awkward when using them.

2 You will need to *overcome mental resistance* to those new behaviors. By overcoming the mental resistance, you will feel emotionally and cognitively comfortable while using the new behavioral norms. You will not feel phony or foolish but respectful and successful.

Learn new behaviors

There are two ways most people learn the new behaviors crucial for cultural adaptation: *cross-cultural training* and *social learning*.

Cross-cultural training

Cross-cultural training is any instructional method, such as instructor-led courses, one-on-one orientations, cultural coaches, online tutorials, or another didactic approach to impart the norms of a different culture. In cross-cultural training, you will likely learn how to interpret the other culture's behaviors, manage expectations for others' behaviors, and respond appropriately with your own behaviors. Often these training sessions offer suggestions for the best behaviors for establishing trust, gaining credibility, and communicating in that culture.

It is best to stagger cross-cultural training in a way that will enable you to debrief challenges as they arise in the novel cultural context. It is only when you are in the context that you will understand how challenging and useful the new behaviors could be.

Consider the example of Anna from earlier in this chapter. A recruiter might have given Anna an explanation of the level of informality of her new employer (the equivalent of training), and likely it would have been easy for Anna to understand the recruiter's message about the difference in norms between her former and new employer. However, it was only when Anna started with the company and had the opportunity to observe norms that she really sensed and felt the difference in organizational cultures. While it is always good to prepare with training, the best time to learn the new culture is when you can observe and practice new behavioral norms in real time, in the new context.

Social learning

Decades of research on social learning, beginning with Alfred Bandura, found that people can learn by observing and imitating the behaviors of role models and being reinforced in the environment for replicating desirable behaviors.[7] Think about the last time you started new job or relocated to a new place for work or school. Chances are you learned the ropes of the new place by observing, talking to people, and testing approaches. You might have had coworkers, neighbors, or classmates take you under their guidance and teach you how to function in the new place.

Over time, you learned what was expected of you and you stopped looking like the newcomer. The environment even rewarded you for fitting in, as Anna was rewarded when she adapted to her new employer's informal culture. At some point, you were able to guess who the newcomers were because they were behaving in a way that was inconsistent with the norms. A tourist cannot easily recognize the difference between a local and a tourist, but a local can with ease.

When in a new country or with people from an unfamiliar cultural context, observe role models, those colleagues who are skilled in working in that country or with people from that culture. Watch how they behave and notice the extent to which those behaviors seem different from ones you would expect. Identify how their behaviors are different from your own. Try to model what they are doing. If you can approach this with a comfortable level of humility and vulnerability, you can even ask them for feedback on how successful you are in exhibiting the behaviors.

Asking for feedback is particularly important when you are unsure of how some of your more subtle behaviors are being perceived and interpreted. After a German colleague and I both gave a talk in Finland, for example, I was surprised how well my German colleague was able to spark a dialogue with the Finnish group. However, when I gave my presentation just after him, I was not as successful in fostering an interaction. I asked a Finnish colleague what I could have done differently. While the Finns' command of English was flawless, she shared that it was difficult for the audience members to understand the subtlety of a questioning tone of voice compared to asking a question more directly. As an American, I only needed an upturned vocal tone at the end of a question to invite a response with an American audience (generally happy to participate). The Finnish colleagues perceived my subtle vocal question as a rhetorical question, not an actual one. She described how, with Finnish audiences, questions needed to be asked more directly and should signal that a response is warranted. It was a wonderful piece of advice based on something I could not observe directly in my own communication style.

Overcoming mental resistance

The greatest pushback I hear from executives when considering the use of cultural adaptation is that they do not like how they feel when behaving differently. They feel disingenuous, embarrassed, or fake when using the behavioral norms of another culture. Merely uttering "when in Rome" does not provide an immediate cognitive or emotional license to behave differently.

Andy Molinsky in his book *Global Dexterity* identified three challenges impeding culturally agile professionals' ability to adapt. They are the feelings of incompetence, lacking authenticity, and resentment. To these I will also add fear of offending, boundary violation, and lack of control. In the next subsections I offer some guidance for how to overcome each of these as you work in situations where cultural adaption is needed.

Overcome feelings of incompetence

While adapting your behaviors might feel awkward at first, it is the key to success in situations requiring this response. Using the training and behavioral modeling discussed in the previous section, you can build your confidence and competence in building a repertoire of diverse behaviors. The more you practice these behaviors, the less self-conscious and more comfortable you will become. Most people can adapt their surface behaviors, such as greetings, communication style, attire, and the like, with relative ease—with practice.

Overcome feelings of inauthenticity

Adapting to aspects of the new culture that do not align with our deeper values poses a mental and emotional challenge. Molinsky describes the authenticity challenge as the conflict you would experience when you are behaving in a way that is counter to your values and beliefs. We feel inauthentic when our behaviors and values are out of alignment, and over time, this can grow into resentment that the situation is suggesting we should be untrue to ourselves.

I would never encourage you to change your values and beliefs. Rather, I encourage you to reframe your interpretations of behaviors and how they align with them. In any new context, you will need to determine whether a certain norm or practice is inappropriate, wrong, inefficient, or even unethical. Once you get to understand the context, however, allow yourself to revise your initial impression if that shift is warranted. Anna, in the prior example, valued professionalism and was able to reframe her perception of informality over time to align with a held value. She started seeing the informality as professionally beneficial, appreciating how the open lines of communication accelerated solutions.

In addition to reframing the new behavior to align with your personal values and beliefs, you can also try a different strategy to maintain authenticity. In this case, you can adapt your behavior only insofar as it still feels authentic. In this way, you create a hybrid between what is fully expected in the local context and your own approach. For example, I am an expressive presenter with a style to match the passion I have for my topic and the desire to be perceived as accessible and warm. My presentation style is consistent with my values. In cultures that are more reserved, my natural high-energy communication style makes me seem bombastic and out of control. I cannot change my style 100 percent and still feel authentic. (I tried and it felt as though I were acting—poorly, at that.) Instead, the hybrid approach worked better to enable me to maintain authenticity: a quieter, more controlled style at first to foster a positive first impression, followed by a more natural, expressive style later in the presentation. This felt better for me, is more effective in reserved cultures, and remains consistent with my values.

Overcome resentment

At the most basic level, the resentment challenge, according to Molinsky, is the sense that one should not need to change behaviors to be accepted by others. This might be a valid feeling, but it is a shortsighted one. Resenting others for having cultural norms and using their subjective judgment to evaluate you is, essentially, resenting them for having functioning limbic systems. Many people can overcome this sense of resentment by actively creating a hybrid approach to behavioral change (as described above). They can also focus on the goal relative to the value of creating behavioral consistency needed to achieve the goal. For example, if you value being friendly and approachable, you might resent being given feedback to act more hierarchical to appear leaderlike if you ever hope to be promoted. Rather than being upset by the feedback, you could process it differently: you value your warmth and approachability because you value open communication. If you want employees in the other culture to communicate with you directly, they first need to establish trust with you. If you use your warmth and approachability too quickly, you might seem shallow, cutting off communication rather than promoting it.

Another way to overcome resentment is to investigate the reason why the behavior is considered more acceptable in that cultural context. You are acting, in a sense, as an objective anthropologist, trying to understand why certain behaviors are preferred in certain cultural contexts. For some people, having this knowledge—and understanding why—is enough to melt resentment and replace it with cognitive understanding.

Overcome the fear of offending others

Oscar Wilde said that "imitation is the sincerest form of flattery." However, in a cross-cultural context, you may feel as though you are not being respectful and flattering. On the contrary, you may feel as though you are being offensive by pretending to act in the way that is considered acceptable in the local environment but not natural to you. You are entitled to your feeling, but this one is largely misplaced. Mirroring behaviors increases a sense of liking and connection between people—rather far from the sense of being offended.

To address this fear directly, Pornpitakpan in her research asked the Thai and Japanese sellers whether the Americans' behavioral adaptation was derogatory and inappropriate. They responded that the feeling was the exact opposite. The Thai and Japanese clients perceived the Americans as "not at all" derogating their culture by using their norms. The negative feeling was only in the mind of the American sellers. The caveat to this is to ensure that you are using the new behavior appropriately. Culturally appropriate behaviors are cringeworthy (and possibly offensive) only when they are overblown or overly exaggerated.

Overcome the feelings of your boundaries being violated

Just as a property boundary would in operate in real estate ownership, personal boundaries delineate what is yours, mine, or shared. Boundaries can be tangible, such as whether food, spaces, or personal items are considered communal or personal. (If you ever had a roommate who ate your food or borrowed your clothes or car without your approval, you might have your own example of this type boundary violation.) Boundary violations can also be sensed more subtly, such as a colleague representing your idea as one that you came up with together or an acquaintance who publicly brings up topics which you believe are private or personal.

People can have either rigid or flexible boundaries, which might vary depending on the issue (e.g., "You can eat my food but do not borrow my clothes" or "I am happy to talk about religion, but political conversations are off limits"). If you have more flexible boundaries, merely understating the cultural norm is usually enough for you to adapt your behavior. However, if you have rigid boundaries about certain things, violations of those boundaries will be difficult to overcome, regardless of the cultural reason for the violation.

In the case of more rigid boundaries, you need to try to communicate your position or find a culturally appropriate way to avoid this boundary being violated. Some culturally agile professionals learn the dance masterfully. One executive who found conversations about politics to be offensive had a conversational go-to strategy which included offering a nonanswer and then changing the subject. A business traveler who could not tolerate cigarette smoke made a habit of finding out where and when most colleagues smoked and then avoided them.

It is possible to hold your boundaries and remain true to yourself while softening your perception of intent. To do this effectively, you will need to hold others with positive regard (i.e., recognize that others did not mean to offend you or violate your personal or emotional space) while developing your strategy to avoid the boundary violation and communicating your preferences with diplomacy.

Overcome the inability to control how you are perceived

In your home cultural context, you can subtly position your responses to foster exactly what you have intended. If you are a well-seasoned professional, predicting how you will be received based on how you are behaving is social intelligence and a sign of your professionalism and executive presence. In an unfamiliar cultural context, we do not have the ability to fine-tune others' responses to us since we are behaving according to norms that we do not know fully. It takes time to learn the full repertoire and regain control over how we appear in that new culture.

Case in point: adapting behaviors during the Covid-19 global pandemic[8]

At the start of the Covid-19 pandemic, I sent my nephew, a hospital-based internal medicine doctor, a text to let him know I was thinking of him. At the end of the text, I added "sending a big hug," my usual Aunt Paula close. "NO HUGGING, AUNT PAULA," he wrote, all caps and a stern-face emoji.

From 1,600 miles away, his text was not meant to be funny. It was a concern-filled directive against my reflexive behavior to hug. My nephew knew how, as a family, we apply social distancing about as well as a basket of puppies. This tactile show of affection, while wonderful for the warm, fuzzy release of oxytocin, became dangerous during the Covid-19 pandemic.

Most everyone comprehended the need for social distancing to limit virus transmission. However, as discussed throughout this book, what we understand can be different from what we do. *Understanding* the directive to change is easy. *Changing* our behavior to be consistent with the new norm is difficult because it is a function of the ingrained response based on what we have learned to be culturally appropriate.

Greetings, social distance, and conversational touching are just a few examples of socialized behaviors that differ across cultures. These behaviors were initially taught to us by parents when we were children; they modeled how we should behave to be socially acceptable. As we matured, the norms our parents taught us were either reinforced and strengthened or diluted and weakened, depending on the norms that were modeled at school, work, with friends, in the communities where we lived, and elsewhere. The stronger the cultural norm, the more difficult it will be to change the behavior. Below are a few examples of social behaviors that required cultural agility to limit the Covid-19 virus transmission.

- *Greetings:* As noted in the chapter on relationship building, everyone has been socialized about how to greet others. Greet with a kiss, a handshake, or a bow.
- *Social distance:* How far we stand from people is also a socialized norm. (Think how "close talkers" make you feel, and you will understand your brain's limbic response to your violated social norm.) During the Covid-19 pandemic, the mandate to keep 6 feet of distance will be easier for those from cultures more comfortable with a greater natural distance.
- *Conversational touching:* For some cultures, it is natural to touch an arm to emphasize a point, connect, or show empathy. There is a wide range of variance in how much touch is used in conversation. Just within Europe, some cultures use touch in conversations eight times more than others.[10]

As we discussed in this chapter, acting in a way that is inconsistent with our cultural norms requires cultural agility, the ability to understand the demands of a novel situation and respond as needed. Even in situations that seem very local (such as the stay-at-home directive during the pandemic), those with cultural agility use a greater level of deliberate, executive functioning to change their behaviors. The new behaviors caused by the pandemic were novel to many around the world, forcing us to change behaviors even in our hometowns.

Using the skills of cultural adaptation, here are some examples that people used to adapt their greeting behaviors. Perhaps you recall using some of these during the pandemic. They included:

- *Share the challenge*. Those in high-touch cultures verbalize how they would like to act but cannot during this time. They say something like "I would love to shake your hand but...," "I want to give you a hug but...," or "I am going to stand over here because..." By expressing the nonnormative behavior, they are giving their brain's reflexive processing a license to change.
- *Create a new cultural norm*. People have adopted behaviors that are new to everyone, more of a cultural integration approach (covered in Chapter 10). For example, elbow bumps and foot taps are two great examples of behaviors that are new to everyone. While the foot taps have not caught on, we saw many people engaging in elbow bumps.
- *Focus on the desired outcome*. Just as in all cases when cultural adaptation is used, we need to move from reflexive, limbic processing to executive, prefrontal cortex processing. One way to do this is to focus on the desired outcome, which, in the case of the pandemic, was to keep everyone as healthy as possible.

How to build your cultural adaptation

The next set of strategies can be used to help you build your cultural adaptation.

- Identify activities which might have a nonnegotiable governing body affecting how you can perform your job or task in the new cultural context. These include any certifications, credentials, licenses, laws, standards, or regulations.
- Before needing to persuade, influence, or lead in a new cultural context, learn how your natural style will be perceived in terms of trustworthiness (e.g., credibility, competence, warmth). Work with coaches, colleagues, or friends who know you and your style well, asking them how you will be

perceived and how you should adapt. Ask for guidance on how to do this and practice or role-play scenarios to master the culturally appropriate behaviors.

- Identify the extent to which the goals you have while in the new cultural context have structured protocols for how they should be achieved. If they do not, identify the best way to achieve the goal in the new cultural context. This might mean asking those who have done the job how they successfully accomplished it (and lessons learned), consulting with cultural coaches who know your goals, and speaking with insiders who know the culture best and have been in a similar situation.
- Engage in social learning around something unrelated to culture (e.g., dancing, cooking, playing Ping-Pong). This will give you the opportunity to practice modeling behavior of others and become comfortable asking for feedback in situations with no professional pressure.

Key takeaways

- There are certain situations where culturally agile professionals need to engage in cultural adaptation, changing their behaviors to match the expected norms of the cultural contexts in which they are working.
- Professional activities needing an advanced level of cultural adaptation are sales, marketing, product relations, and product development for local markets.
- To be effective in cultural adaptation, culturally agile professionals need to master the skills of learning new, culturally appropriate behaviors and overcoming mental resistance to using those new behaviors.
- To learn new behaviors for cultural adaptation, engage in cross-cultural training and social learning.
- To overcome mental resistance while using cultural adaptation, you will need to address any feelings of incompetence, lack of authenticity, resentment, fear of offending, boundary violation, and lack of control over how you are being perceived.

Keep reading

- Meyer, E. 2014. *The Culture Map: Breaking through the Invisible Boundaries of Global Business*. New York: Public Affairs.
- Molinsky, A. 2013. *Global Dexterity: How to Adapt Your Behavior across Cultures without Losing Yourself in the Process*. Boston: Harvard Business Review Press.
- Trompenaars, F., and Hampden-Turner, C. 2012. *Riding the Waves of Culture: Understanding Diversity in Global Business*, 3rd ed. New York: McGraw-Hill Education.

Endnotes

1 Caligiuri, P., and Bonache, J. 2020. "The Non-Linear Relationships in Cross-Cultural Management and Global Mobility." In *The SAGE Handbook of Contemporary Cross-Cultural Management*, ed. B. Szkudlarek, L. Romani, D. V. Caprar, and J. S. Osland. Thousand Oaks, CA: SAGE.

2 Augustine. The Confessions and Letters of St. Augustine. Letter 54 (Book 1: Replies to Questions of Januarius), 2.3. https://www.ccel.org/ccel/schaff/npnf101.vii.1.LIV.html#vii.1.LIV-p10 (archived at https://perma.cc/494K-JU6V) [Accessed September 30, 2020].

3 Weck, M., and Ivanova, M. 2013. "The Importance of Cultural Adaptation for the Trust Development within Business Relationships." *Journal of Business and Industrial Marketing* 28, no. 3: 210–220.

4 A sample of these studies includes: Pornpitakpan, C. 2004. "The Effect of Americans' Adaptation to Malaysians on Perceived Trustworthiness." *Journal of International Consumer Marketing* 16: 7–23; Pornpitakpan, C. 1999. "The Effects of Cultural Adaptation on Business Relationships: Americans Selling to Japanese and Thais." *Journal of International Business Studies* 30: 317–337; Pornpitakpan, C. 1997. "The Effect of Cultural Adaptation on Perceived Trustworthiness." *Journal of International Consumer Marketing* 15: 25–41.

5 Shin, S. J., Morgeson, F. P., and Campion, M. A. 2007. "What You Do Depends on Where You Are: Understanding How Domestic and Expatriate Work Requirements Depend upon the Cultural Context." *Journal of International Business Studies* 38, no. 1: 64–83.

6 Hirst, G., Budhwar, P., Cooper, B., West, M., Long, C., Chongyuan, X., and Shipton, H. 2008. "Cross-Cultural Variations in Climate for Autonomy, Stress and Organizational Productivity Relationships: A Comparison of Chinese and

UK Manufacturing Organizations." *Journal of International Business Studies* 39: 1343–1358.

7 For more information on social learning theory: Bandura, A. 1986. *Social Foundations of Thought and Action: A Social Cognitive Theory*. Englewood Cliffs, NJ: Prentice-Hall; Bandura, A. 1977. *Social Learning Theory*. Englewood Cliffs, NJ: Prentice Hall.

8 Caligiuri, P. April 29, 2020. "Say Goodbye to Handshakes and Hugs." Entrepreneurship & Innovation Exchange. https://eiexchange.com/content/say-goodbye-to-handshakes-and-hugs (archived at https://perma.cc/3YBR-4JXZ) [Accessed September 23, 2020].

9 Sorokowska, A., Sorokowski, P., Hilpert, P., Cantarero, K., et al. 2017. "Preferred Interpersonal Distances: A Global Comparison." *Journal of Cross-Cultural Psychology* 48, no. 4: 577–592.

10 Remland, M., Jones, T., and Brinkman, H. 1995. "Interpersonal Distance, Body Orientation, and Touch: Effects of Culture, Gender, and Age." *Journal of Social Psychology* 135, no. 3: 281–297.

Cultural minimization to uphold a standard in a culturally diverse situation 09

Cultural minimization

The cultural response Kim needed to enable Rumi Spice to be success on the global market is cultural minimization. Culturally agile professionals, like Kim, who engage in cultural minimization can hold a standard, achieve a superordinate goal, or create greater consistency even when doing so might mean operating in a way that is inconsistent with the cultural norm.

There are a variety of jobs and roles most often requiring cultural minimization to be successful, including health and safety, quality assurance, strategic company-wide practices, global reputation or brand consistency, production schedules, operations, and many others. In Kim's case, she knew that Rumi Spice, to be successful, would need to follow global standards for quality and purity. Even though uniforms, workstations, and a sterile environment were not consistent with Afghan norms, she was able to accomplish the goal.

Many organizations fall short on creating consistency around the world even when doing so is consistent with strategic and growth initiatives. Generally, I can spot examples of this problem when I see translated policy documents or standard training sessions implemented around the world.

These initiatives often cover issues such as health and safety standards, codes of conduct, diversity and inclusion, quality standards, fiscal controls, corporate values, and codes of ethics. These initiatives often fail.

In many years of working with global professionals, I have found that they frequently describe executing a task requiring cultural minimization as one of the most challenging of their careers; the difficulty is almost always a function of a lack of understanding of the cultural norms impeding implementation. Universally, people do not like to change their natural behaviors and certainly will not do so just because a policy hangs on a poster in the break room or they were required to attend a training class.

Cultural minimization starts with a deep understanding of how the cultural context can affect your desired outcome; this is only fully understood by "insiders" who have been socialized within that context and understand it fully. It will always be difficult as a cultural outsider (even the most culturally agile among us) to identify the trip wires associated with cultural minimization, but it is a necessary first step. To create a standard, local knowledge from a trusted cultural insider is critical. Rely on your network of colleagues, cultural coaches, and mentors.

To succeed in a situation requiring cultural minimization, you will need to develop a tangible strategy to shape the behaviors of colleagues, vendors, partners, suppliers, associates, and subordinates once the cross-cultural context is fully understood. Through direct and indirect influence, use a more nuanced approach to *socialization, persuasion*, and *motivation* to encourage others to adhere to the new countercultural behaviors.

Socialization

Recall the last time you started new job or began at a new school. Did you go through a formal orientation process? Or were you on your own to learn the ropes through observing, asking questions, and trying approaches until you learned what was appropriate for the new context? You might have had coworkers, neighbors, or classmates take you under their wings and teach you how "things are done around here." Maybe you made mistakes and your behavior was corrected. Maybe the rules were so strict and overtly communicated that the behaviors expected of you were easily understood. However you were socialized, when using the expected behaviors, you began fitting in, and it was no longer obvious to others that you were the newcomer. In fact, you so deeply understood the expected behaviors that you were able to identify the newbies, those who had not yet learned the norms. You had become fully *socialized.*

While everyone has been socialized at some point in their life (e.g., where to return the crayons in kindergarten, where to place your tray in the lunchroom cafeteria), far fewer have experienced actively socializing others, especially in a professional, countercultural context. This is a skill, a practiced act, requiring five interlocking strategies. Let's consider each.

Adapt communication to the local context

Communicating the expected norm might mean that you need to use a different form of verbal or nonverbal communication. The message remains the same but you will need to change the way the message is delivered. In a study comparing the messaging effectiveness of a global corporate-wide safety practices in three subsidiaries (the US, France, and Argentina), the same message had different perceptions.[1] The expected norms within the US-based policy were identical. However, the Argentinean workers viewed the safety practices in an acceptable, more paternalistic manner; they believed their company (and the managers) had a sincere concern for their safety. The French workers, in contrast, did not readily see the top-down communicated policy as a concern for personal safety. They were suspicious of the corporate approach and would have been more receptive if a team of fellow workers was the conduit of the message. The same impassioned safety speech from an American leader, while motivating the Argentinean workers, would elicit cynical eye rolls from the French workers.

This example also underscores that you might need to, at times, select a different messenger. This is especially the case if you do not have the deepest grasp of the verbal, nonverbal, and cultural nuances of the context. It might also be the case if the cultural context you are in does not perceive you as trusted or credible. As Kim experienced as a female military leader in Afghanistan, know how you (the messenger) will affect how the message will be received. Do not take this step personally—which is easier said than done. Keep your eye on the superordinate goal, as Kim did when she asked her male subordinate to communicate with the Afghan leaders.

Train on the expectations of subjective norms

I have spent many hours with executives working through the culturally subjective aspects of their global initiatives. Their blind spot is always the same: When a policy, practice, or strategy is crystal clear to those developing the initiative, even if they represent a diverse group of corporate leaders, it does not have a shared meaning in subsidiaries around the world. The group of corporate leaders is oftentimes so deeply embedded in the corporate culture that they have a limited collective ability to process the range of possible ways a subjective goal could be interpreted across cultures. Senior leaders, regardless of their country of origin, often share values and interpret subjective meanings the same way. These initiatives take hold in headquarters, where they were created, but fall flat around the world.

Corporate values are almost always the thorniest to trot out globally. For example, consider the sentence from a typical American corporate values statement: "We value authenticity and diversity." Authenticity is a concept widely understood among those who have been socialized in individualistic contexts but less meaningful to those from collectivistic cultures. Diversity is defined differently, depending on where you are in the world. If you are implementing an initiative or policy, these subjective concepts will need to be made objective with clear behavioral examples. What exactly does "valuing authenticity" mean? What exactly does "valuing diversity" mean?

To address this you will need to identify a culturally appropriate way to offer behavioral training. For example, instead of just emphasizing the importance of customer responsiveness, define what you mean by customer responsiveness. "Every customer will receive a response within ten minutes of any inquiry" provides greater guidance than "respond to customers promptly." The word *promptly* is subjective. Define everything behaviorally.

Attract, select, and retain those who behave in accordance with the norm

Be certain that any countercultural behaviors are fully understood by those applying for positions in your organization. In recruitment activities, share the corporate behaviors clearly so future employees can opt out of working for your company if it would mean changing behaviors that they have no intention of changing. Likewise, you might find that some people are differentially attracted to working for your organization *because of* a shared value. They already ascribe to the norm, even though it is not typical in their own cultural context.

Remember that while companies often talk about values, they are often more interested in the behaviors (not the values) of their employees. Values are deeply held principles of how one sees the world. They foster attitudes and guide how individuals prioritize the facets of their lives, how they interact with others, and how they relate to their organization or society. Values and attitudes can shift, but they do so very slowly, through deep socialization. They are the "why" people do what they do. For example, your company might have global nonnegotiable standards against any form of sexual harassment form. However, policing lewd jokes an employee shares with a friend at home would be beyond your purview. (It is okay to hope that the socialization from your organization will, over time, shift the employee's attitude about lewd jokes. We can hope.)

In cultural minimization, your expected behaviors are nonnegotiable if there is a countercultural initiative which is core to how your organization competes globally. Select these carefully (not everything needs cultural minimization) and find the contextually appropriate way to exit those who are not behaving accordingly. In the United States, firing employees is easier than in many other countries, as Americans are considered "at will" employees with few legal protections. The ability to fire an employee is much more difficult in most other countries. The bottom line here is to select critical countercultural behaviors, those which are truly nonnegotiable, carefully.

Reinforce behaviors in a culturally appropriate way

When you are engaging in a cultural minimization response, you want to reward behavioral change. Keep in mind, however, that there are cultural differences in what people perceive as reinforcing rewards.[2] For example, people from more individualistic cultures respond to individual-level visible rewards, such as praise, perks, or recognition. Being singled out as doing well feels good for those from individualistic cultures. This is not the case in more collectivistic cultures, which tend to respond to group-level rewards, such as a team recognition. Similarly, in hierarchical cultures, receiving a request from one's boss would be more likely to change behavior compared to those from egalitarian cultures who do not value higher positions as being the most credible authority. Peer recognition might be more appropriate in egalitarian cultures. We will revisit these cultural differences in the motivation section below.

Model the norm

Even if you do not have formal position power, if are you someone others respect, regardless of culture, your behaviors will be emulated. When your behaviors are emulated, you naturally help facilitate situations requiring cultural minimization. At the most basic level, be certain you are consistently modeling the norms you expect in others.

According to the extensive GLOBE (Global Leadership and Organizational Behavior Effectiveness) Study, a large-scale assessment of cultural and leadership differences across sixty-two countries, there are universal behaviors which make people appear more leaderlike.[3] They include being visionary, inspirational, decisive, performance-oriented, diplomatic, team-oriented, and having high integrity. You will still need to learn how to exhibit these correctly in the culture within which you are working, but they are a good place to start everywhere in the world.

Persuasion

In addition to leveraging the above methods of socialization, you will want to use your skills of persuasion and influence to foster new behaviors. Ping Ping Fu and her colleagues from around the world conducted an extensive study on cross-national differences in the effectiveness of influence and persuasion strategies.[4] They found that individuals' cultural values affect how various influence tactics are perceived. For those who believe that life's events are predetermined by fate and destiny, being an assertive and coercive authority is perceived as more effective for influencing compared to liking someone with whom one has a positive social relationship. For those from group-oriented cultures, positive social relationships and liking enable a more effective influence strategy.

In addition to understanding the context in which you need to be persuasive, Robert Cialdini, the leading researcher on the topic of influence and persuasion, identified six universal principles that can be used to shape the behaviors of others.[5] As universal principles, they have worked in a variety of cultural contexts.

Reciprocation

Reciprocation is the desire to keep parity in our relationships such that we are all motivated to repay favors when someone does something for us. You can try to implement this for cultural minimization if you can offer something at work prior to the request for the behavioral change. The challenge in using this strategy is to make it personal, and it will likely only work in one-on-one relationships.

Commitment and consistency

We as humans like to maintain consistency with our values and behaviors. We tend to make decisions and then amplify our behaviors that will be perceived as consistent with those decisions. If you can begin to shift behaviors in a small but meaningful way, you might be able to dial up the behavioral commitment as people want to remain consistent with what they first agreed to do. For example, signing a pledge to act in a certain manner would be an initial commitment. The behaviors requested to follow that commitment would be the consistency.

Creating a social norm

We are social animals so we will look to others we believe are like us for clues on what we should be doing. To use this successfully in cultural minimization, try to identify individuals' referent groups. Then try to make a case for the behavior by broadcasting the mass adoption of the behavior. For example, if another subsidiary has already adopted a certain behavior, show their results in adopting that behavior along with the positive outcome.

Liking

We will naturally be persuaded more by people we naturally like. Liking, however, can have some cultural nuances, as described in Chapter 9 on relationship building. Try to find a way to be viewed as likable in the culture in which you are working.

Authority

Much like the previous method on liking, we tend to be persuaded when we view someone as the authority on the topic, someone who has a high level of expertise or experience. In many cases, it is helpful to find experts who are from the culture and understand how to demonstrate their authority in a culturally appropriate way. The strategy is ineffective if the authority on the topic is not perceived as credible within the cultural context.

Scarcity

We tend to desire the things we believe are of limited availability. (Do we all remember the run on toilet paper during the coronavirus global pandemic?)

This might be a less useful strategy in cultural minimization, but you could try offering "limited seating" for a key training program around a desired behavior. You might find people seeking it out for reasons of scarcity (and then, hopefully, the principle of consistency will kick in).

Motivation

Being able to effectively encourage individuals to do the things they might not have otherwise been inclined to do means that you are motivating their behaviors. Increasing quality, improving punctuality, or more closely adhering to a policy are examples of motivating behaviors for cultural minimization. When you are motivating others, you are encouraging them to act in way that will help achieve a specific goal, in return for something they desire. The desirable thing might be an intangible, such as praise, a sense of belonging, or feelings of personal development, or something tangible, such as a bonus, extra vacation days, or a gift card for a cup of coffee.

We have all been motivated by others at some point in our lives. You can probably recall coaches, teachers, bosses, colleagues, or classmates who were able to get more effort from you while making you feel great about expending the effort. They understood you well enough to know what tangible or intangible reward you would find motivating and encouraged your behavior with that reward.

The challenge of motivating others, especially in a cross-cultural context, is that people are not necessarily motivated by the same things. For example, public praise for excellence might be highly motivating for those in more individualistic cultures whereas the same public praise might be considered embarrassing for those from a collectivistic culture. The good news is that there are four universal motivators that, when applied correctly in the cross-cultural context, can be extremely successful everywhere.[6] For most people, irrespective of culture, when they are receiving one or more of these four things, they will continue the behavior. They are:

- Create meaning and a connection to purpose.
- Provide opportunities for mastery and self-efficacy.
- Provide a sense of ownership through autonomy or responsibility.
- Foster connectedness and a sense of membership.

Understanding these four universal motivators is a great start. They are like tools in a toolbox that can be used in situations where cultural minimization is needed. The challenge is knowing when and how you use the tools in a culturally appropriate way. When you work across cultures, meaning, support, sense of ownership, belonging—all can mean different things to people and can be achieved in different ways. Knowing how they might vary will help you create a portfolio of different ways to motivate behaviors.

Create meaning and a connection to purpose

Did you ever watch the faces of people who are volunteering in the aftermath of a natural disaster? Whether they are searching for survivors, providing medical care, or aiding in a rescue, look at their faces. They have an unparalleled look of determination as they work tirelessly with heroic effort. Universally, you will see the same look of raw commitment to the cause. It is the sense of meaning or purpose propelling the herculean effort.

Giving your employees a greater connection to the work they are doing (and the behaviors you are asking them to adapt) will help motivate behaviors. While not as dramatic as a rescue mission, you can connect employees to the stories of customers, clients, patients, students, or any of those who will ultimately be connected to the company. The deeper sense of meaning you can create will provide better results. For example, quality at an auto manufacturing plant might be connected to customer safety. In creating meaning and a sense of purpose, however, tailor the message to the culture. In some cultures, appealing to emotions is more motivating; in others, the facts will be the more powerful motivator.

Provide opportunities for mastery and self-efficacy

Most people are motivated to feel as though they are developing in competence around something of importance. To help motivate behaviors as others are learning them, be sure you coach in a way that is appreciated in that culture. The greatest mistake leaders make when managing globally is to underestimate the importance of direct versus indirect feedback.

In low-context communication cultures, giving direct feedback is appreciated because it shows a commitment to one's improvement (i.e., "You care enough about me to provide me with straight direction and correction"). In high-context cultures, that same direct feedback can be demotivating, even if it was well meaning, because it feels more offensive and hurtful. In these cultures, try a more subtle form of feedback and provide resources for development, like training classes.

Provide a sense of ownership through autonomy or responsibility

While it is universally motivating to be provided with autonomy, what is considered autonomy in one culture might be poor leadership (or abandonment) in another. Saying something like "I trust you to figure it out" could inspire confidence in someone from a more individually oriented culture. You believe in her. That is motivating. Say the same thing to someone from a more collectivist culture and you might be viewed as irresponsible. Providing autonomy in a more collectivist situation means providing the support and resources for someone to achieve independently.

The same is true for power. Giving someone power, say through a promotion, is motivating for some. In more hierarchical societies, like Eastern European countries, people are motivated by power. They want to manage or lead. But in more egalitarian societies, such as Scandinavian countries, this need for power is lower, and so this will not be as powerful of a motivator.

Foster connectedness and a sense of membership

One of the most fundamental human desires is to feel as though we belong to and are accepted by a group. We *want* to belong. But, as you have probably already guessed, the meaning of belonging depends on the culture. In task-oriented cultures, people tend to appreciate being a member of a team that is known as high-performing. They want to know that they are a star among other stars. In more relationship-orientated cultures, that sense of belonging is created when individuals feel as though they are working in a trusted environment with people they care about—and who care for them. Either way, feeling like a valued member of a group makes us want to do more. In a task-oriented culture, reinforce the desired behaviors by calling out team successes. In a relationship-orientated culture, reward with social events and other ways to foster team connection and trust.

Case in point: Shell's Global Zero Work Site Hazard Project

Graham Robinson put cultural minimization approaches into action as the manager of Shell's Global Zero Work Site Hazard Project. In this role, he had a goal to ensure future safety at Shell globally and reinforce safety practices and culture everywhere in the world. Safety is nonnegotiable for Shell, fundamental to the company's core values, so any cultural variation in these behaviors needed to be minimized. Robinson described Goal Zero as "a change programme aimed at regions was implemented, and visible recognition for exemplary safety performance and celebration of 'zero days' were carried out. In addition, a zero tolerance policy was adopted for people who create conditions that endanger lives."[7] As an example of socialization, Shell adopted a zero-tolerance policy such that anyone who refused to follow all safety protocol was not allowed to remain with the organization. The strong and swift action quickly shaped global safety practices.

At the same time, culturally appropriate methods of persuasion and motivation were also used. For example, to foster acceptance for Shell's safety program in Indonesia, Darwin Silalahi, country chairman and CEO, reiterated the nonnegotiable Shell safety practices but appealed to the Indonesian collectivist values. "At Shell, we believe we are all safety leaders. What each of us does individually results in our collective culture. We must each take personal responsibility for creating a culture of compliance and intervention."[8] Mr. Silalahi created a cultural minimization strategy but also leveraged knowledge of culture values. This approach resonated with the group-oriented Indonesians.

How to build your cultural minimization

Successfully implementing a strategy requiring cultural minimization takes time, cultural understanding, and planning. Appropriate socialization, persuasion, and motivation methods are universal but will always be more effective when they are implemented with an understanding of the cultural nuances. Here are some suggestions for building the skills needed for cultural minimization.

- Many people who are drawn to cross-cultural work find asking others to conform their behaviors in a countercultural way to be uncomfortable. Implementing a response which requires cultural minimization requires practice and a development of skills. It will get easier as you foster the ability to express humility and respect for the culture while maintaining the standards needed to enable success. Try practicing these so you are ready when a cross-cultural situation requires cultural minimization.
- Identify the specific practices in your organization that are nonnegotiable from the perspective of the organization's desire to maintain consistency

around the world. Health and safety standards, codes of conduct, quality standards, fiscal controls, corporate values, and codes of ethics are typical examples of activities companies typically wish to standardize and control worldwide. Research how well these standards have been met around the world.

- Interview those with responsibility for global implementation of a standard to see what worked (and what did not) during the implementation. It is helpful to ask your interviewees: What would they do differently to have an even greater acceptance? What surprised them?—either in what did work or what did not work. Usually these lessons are quite powerful.
- Be more observant of subjective norms in your organization. Do this by identifying the values, policies, or strategies that are widely accepted in your organization but are, in fact, more subjective. What is the range of interpretations one could have for something which is widely accepted as a corporate value? This skill will help you be the one who continually asks, "Does everyone understand this the same way?"
- Practice influence strategies mentioned in this chapter (i.e., reciprocation, creating commitment and consistency, creating a social norm, liking, authority, and scarcity). Are any of them more natural for you? Do you have a few dominant persuasion methods? Try to alter your style across different situations, practicing those methods that might be less comfortable.
- Practice the motivation strategies in this chapter (i.e., creating meaning and a connection to purpose, providing opportunities for mastery, providing a sense of ownership through autonomy, and fostering connectedness and a sense of membership). Do any of these come more naturally than others?
- Cultural minimization requires that you see the cross-cultural differences and at the same time encourage others to change their behaviors through socialization, motivation, and persuasion. There are two important skills to practice. First, gain an understanding of cultural differences in the desired behavior. Second, gain an understanding of how to successfully change the behavior. Practice these in low-risk professional or volunteer situations.

Key takeaways

- There are certain situations where culturally agile professionals need to engage in cultural minimization, reducing the role of cultural differences to uphold a standard or adhere to a regulation or value.
- Professional activities needing an advanced level of cultural minimization are safety, production, operations, logistics, and ethics.
- To be effective in cultural minimization, culturally agile professionals need to master the skills of socialization, persuasion, and motivation.
- To socialize behavior in cultural minimization, culturally agile professionals will need to communicate and socially reinforce in a culturally nuanced way, provide a frame of reference for subjective expectations, and enable attraction-selection-retention to shape expected behaviors.
- To influence behavior in cultural minimization, the six universal principles of persuasion (reciprocation, commitment and consistency, creating a social norm, liking, authority, and scarcity) should be used in culturally appropriate ways.
- To motivate behavior, the four motivators (sense of purpose, mastery, autonomy, and growth) should be used in culturally appropriate ways.

Keep reading

- Cialdini, R. 2018. *Pre-Suasion: A Revolutionary Way to Influence and Persuade*. New York: Simon & Schuster.
- Cialdini, R. 2006. *Influence: The Psychology of Persuasion*. New York: Simon & Schuster.
- Coyle, D. 2018. *The Culture Code: The Secrets of Highly Successful Groups*. New York: Bantam Books.
- Pink, D. 2011. *Drive: The Surprising Truth about What Motivates Us*. New York: Riverhead Books.
- Sinek, S. 2011. *Start with Why: How Great Leaders Inspire Everyone to Take Action*. New York: Portfolio.

Endnotes

1 Janssens, M., Brett, J., and Smith, F. 1995. "Confirmatory Cross-Cultural Research Testing the Viability of a Corporation-Wide Safety Policy." *Academy of Management Journal* 38, no. 2: 364–382.

2 Olsen, J. 2015. "Societal Values and Individual Values in Reward Allocation Preferences." *Cross Cultural Management* 22, no. 2: 187–200.

3 House, R. J., Hanges, P. J., Javidan, M., Dorfman, P. W., and Gupta, V., eds. 2004. *Culture, Leadership, and Organizations: The GLOBE Study of 62 Societies*. Thousand Oaks, CA: SAGE.

4 Fu, P. P., Kennedy, J., Tata, J., Yukl, G., Bond, M.H., Peng, T. K., Srinivas, E. S., et al. 2004. "The Impact of Societal Cultural Values and Individual Social Beliefs on the Perceived Effectiveness of Managerial Influence Strategies: A Meso Approach." *Journal of International Business Studies* 35, no. 4: 284–305.

5 Cialdini, R. B. 2006. *Influence: The Psychology of Persuasion*. New York: Harper Business.

6 Deci, E. L., and Ryan, R.M. 2000. "The 'What' and 'Why' of Goal Pursuits: Human Needs and the Self-Determination of Behavior." *Psychological Inquiry* 11: 227–268.

7 Goal Zero marks change in HSE mindset for Shell. "Drilling Contractor." September 20, 2008. www.drillingcontractor.org/goal_zero_marks_change_in_hse_mindset_for_shell-691 (archived at https://perma.cc/56PE-FY2F).

8 Hidayat, T. "Darwin Silalahi: Aiming to Become a Memorable Leader," The Jakarta Post, August 22, 2007.

10 Cultural integration to create new norms for group success in a culturally diverse situation

Cultural adaptation (Chapter 8) and cultural minimization (Chapter 9) are two possible responses or task management competencies when working in different countries or with people from different cultures. As discussed, you use the cultural adaptation response whenever you need to align your behaviors to the expected norms of those with whom you are interacting. You will likely be using this response when the power in the relationship favors the other culture (e.g., the buyer, the regulatory body, or government). At the other end of the continuum, you will use the cultural minimization response when you need to uphold a standard because it is consistent with strategic goals, quality standards, accounting rules, codes of ethics, health and safety practices, and the like. This chapter covers the third, and final, task management competency: **cultural integration**.

Cultural integration is required anytime the creation of an entirely new set of norms is needed to increase buy-in from people in different countries or from different cultures. While potentially time-consuming, cultural integration fosters a new hybrid approach which does not represent any one culture's preferred response or behavioral norms. Successful cultural integration means that the resulting entity—whether a new organizational policy or the creation of a global team's operating norms—will not overrepresent any of the cultures involved, unless that is what the group determines is best. Solutions are negotiated and considered acceptable (or equally unacceptable) to everyone involved. It is about compromise—and a healthy amount of diplomacy.

Situations requiring cultural integration

Cultural integration is often leveraged in any situation requiring people from diverse cultures to create an entirely new set of norms which does not overrepresent the preference of any one country or culture. Here are some scenarios in which cultural integration is used:

- As a *global virtual team* forms, the team members collaborate to create their own rules for interactions, set their collective expectations for information sharing, design their own communication approaches, and create their team identity. Cultural integration is often used by successful global teams to create a hybrid team culture, unique to each team, that will facilitate the teams' functioning.
- Two colleagues of different cultures need to engage in *conflict resolution* after their differences in working styles affect their ability to work together effectively. In this case, each one's perceptions of the other's behaviors are being misperceived and misconstrued, leading to conflict. The colleagues use cultural integration to determine the best way to collaborate and share information in the future.
- A company *introducing a company-wide practice* convenes the colleagues who understand the challenges associated with the practice from their respective culture, functional area, or generation. Together, the colleagues compromise to create a practice that will work for the entire company but does not overrepresent any one preferred way of doing things. In situations requiring the creation of a global policy, practice, or standard, cultural integration brings together many diverse perspectives to create a solution with the greatest chance for success everywhere.
- Two companies come together through a *merger, acquisition, or joint venture*. Leaders from each company work together to retain the values from each entity while creating and enacting a new strategy.

Across these diverse examples, the common element is the need to convene, communicate, compromise, and create something new. That short sentence is fraught with challenges and often requires the guidance of facilitators, coaches, or leader.

If you are in a leadership role, you might be in the position of facilitator or coach to create the psychological safety necessary for cultural integration to occur. This means that you will need to create an environment that allows everyone to feel respected and to be vulnerable as they offer opinions and ideas, challenge each other, and take risks without personal or professional consequences.

An example of this type of leadership in cultural integration was evident in the period leading up to the Lenovo acquisition of IBM's PC Division. Before the acquisition, Yuanqing Yang, the chairman of Lenovo, and Steve Ward, the president, created certain ground rules for the acquisition based on three guiding principles for the entire company to follow: candor, respect, and compromise. Their leadership at the top created an environment of psychological safety and facilitated open communication and collaboration.

Yang and Ward also chose their cultural battles carefully; they did not try to impose a consistent approach throughout the organization, using cultural minimization, unless one was absolutely needed. Similarly, these leaders did not use cultural integration if doing so was not practical or strategically necessary. In his own words, in a keynote address for the Academy of International Business, Chuan Zhi Liu, CEO and president of the Legend Holdings Ltd. (the parent company that acquired Lenovo), spoke about the philosophy that guided cultural integration throughout the acquisition, describing how they promoted common interests and cultural integration by focusing on only those issues that were essential. He said, "We divided issues into significant and inconsequential ones. For the latter, we felt that there was no point in wasting time and energy on them, so that we could focus our attention on the significant issues that need to be addressed."[1]

This strategy was successful. Today, Lenovo remains one of the world's largest sellers of personal computers and has successfully used this approach to engage in many more strategic acquisitions, such as a 51 percent stake in Fujitsu's personal computer division.[2]

As Chuan Zhi Liu noted, cultural integration is not to be applied in every situation because it does take time and energy to create new behavioral norms. Using resources to convene, communicate, compromise, and create new approaches is sometimes not worth the effort. This is especially true in situations where either the headquarters' approach (cultural minimization) or a local approach (cultural adaptation) would be more appropriate. As with the other cultural responses, you will need to select when to invest the resources to employ cultural integration. Choose your battles wisely.

Skills needed for cultural integration

Whether creating a better working relationship with a coworker from a different culture or facilitating a successful merger between companies headquartered in different countries, you will need to know how to comfortably discuss behavioral differences before you can start to work toward a culturally integrated approach. *Comfortable* is an important word here. Having an open dialogue about behavioral differences can be thorny and, if not handled well, can produce animosity. Many well-meaning cultural integration approaches were stopped cold because compromise is not possible when someone is communicating defensively.

Here are some skills you can master to be better equipped to engage in cultural integration.

Learn about potential differences before you begin dialogue

Learn as much as you can about any potential cultural differences you might experience. This is a good time to activate your network of cultural guides to better understand how to interpret cross-cultural behaviors more accurately. As discussed in Chapter 8, the two ways most people learn how to interpret cross-cultural behaviors is cross-cultural training and social learning. These remain as critical for cultural integration as they do for the other two responses.

Set a positive tone

If you begin a communication, notice if people are uncomfortable, unresponsive, or defensive when discussing cultural differences. If you sense this, do not move forward. Stop. Spend more time establishing trust in the group, which might mean investing in a team-building social event or just taking a short break and coming back to remind everyone of the overarching goal. Try to foster trust first and then position the conversation as a more collaborative one. If there is some trust, you can position the collaboration with a comment such as "We have so many excellent working styles that have made us each effective in our own culture. Since we all work a bit differently, let's create how we want to work together." Keep the focus on potential differences as positives.

In setting a positive tone, do your best to allow everyone involved to identify the strengths and weaknesses of his or her own approach. In other words, allow everyone to surface their own criticisms. If trust has been created, this will feel objective rather than defensive. Using this approach, you can also help create the tacit understanding that there is no one best way to do things.

Focus on behaviors

Defensiveness during cultural integration conversations tends to arise when people sense that their values are being negatively evaluated. No one with a healthy sense of identity will want to compromise his or her underlying values—or have them questioned. To avoid this trip wire, be certain you keep the conversation about observable behaviors and approaches and not the perception of the meaning underlying them. If you focus on behaviors, you will sense a greater willingness to compromise because behaviors, unlike values, change more readily as situations change. In fact, there is only a modest correlation between attitudes and behaviors because people can and do adapt their behavioral responses to their circumstances.[3]

To remain focused on that which you can observe, you will need to work on (and practice) describing behavioral differences without any value judgments associated. Remember, this is difficult because we will need to override our subjective brain's super-speedy processor. For example:

- Rather than accusing your time-fluid colleague of being unprofessional, state that the agreed-upon deadline was not met.
- Rather than interpreting your task-oriented colleagues as being cold or aloof, identify that the time spent in relationship building varies within your work group, and that, in the context of the present team, some time spent on relationship-building can be valuable for team effectiveness.
- Rather than saying that the practice in a certain country is inefficient because it takes too long to render a decision, describe how you need to better understand the rationale for the steps in each country's process.

Focus on the behaviors and not the values underlying expressed behaviors. Encourage others to do the same. We see this challenge in a different type of cultural difference—the generational difference. Here is a typical scenario that often needs cultural integration: You need to create a more effective way for a multigenerational team to share information. Using subjective negative judgments, the younger teammates complain that the older teammates are too rigid (negative, subjective) because they want too many unnecessary (negative, subjective) in-person meetings (objective). The older teammates see the younger generations as lacking commitment (negative, subjective) because they send short communications throughout the day (objective) and show up to meetings unprepared (negative, subjective) with no way to even take notes. The team members from both generations are likely flexible and committed, but their working preferences were socialized differently. Older generations "went to work" during a fixed time during the day while the younger generations "do work" asynchronously to fit the task.[4]

Recognizing these differences and leveraging cultural integration, a multigenerational team can focus on behaviors and set some basic ground rules on how to share information in a way that merges the older generation's desire to convene and the younger generation's desire to be responsive.

Cultural integration in global teams

The most pervasive need for cultural integration that I have seen is among **interdependent teams** with team members who are from different cultures, generations, functional areas, and the like. Interdependent teams are those in which the members need to rely on each other to accomplish their overarching goal as a team. They are not merely colocated. They do not just pass work along. They need to coordinate their work. The greater the interdependence, the greater the need for cultural integration.

The best example of the difference in interdependence of teams is from professional sports. Research has found that star athletes can be detrimental to the performance of a team because they do not necessarily feel the need to be integrated with the rest of the team. This "lone star" concern is more problematic in some sports than in others, based on their level of interdependence. Professional soccer and basketball teams suffer more from unintegrated elite players compared to professional baseball teams because, in baseball, the players do not need a high level of coordination to win games.[5] Incidentally, it is interesting to note that Major League Baseball in the United States has tremendous cultural diversity; roughly 30 percent of players were not born in the United States, compared to the National Football League with less than 5 percent foreign players.

It is likely that most of your teams will function more like basketball or soccer teams, with a greater level of interdependence. For this reason, it is well worth your effort to engage in cultural integration because diverse teams function better when they create a hybrid team culture with its own unique norms for interactions, communications, goal setting, and the like.[6] These culturally integrated teams establish their own rules for interpersonal and task-related interactions, their own expectations for performance management, their own preferences for effective communication and conflict resolution, and their own identity.

Here are five suggestions for fostering cultural integration in your diverse team.

Start strong

Whenever possible, meet in person as the team is forming. Remember how trust is formed among individuals. We trust those with whom we believe we have something in common. If we spend some time at the beginning of the team's formation to get to know one another, it is likely the team members will find some similarity, such as a sport, a hobby, a favorite vacation spot, or even the same birthday.

Be certain to create a team charter and team ground rules. Elements to include are response speed (e.g., how long it should take to respond to an email). The group should also agree upon work styles that tend to have wide variation, such as response tone (brief or longer) and who should be included in what decisions (i.e., when to include the manager). Practical aspects of working together should also be agreed upon, such as how the team will share information, how frequently the team will meet, and the like.

There is another benefit to spending time to get to know the other members of the team: creating a sense of congruence. This means that, in general, people want to be seen by others in a way that is consistent with their own beliefs about themselves. They feel congruent in the sense that they are perceived to be authentic, understood, and validated by their team members. According to research, when team members created this sense of congruence, the team's diversity *enhanced* the team's performance.[7]

However, the team's diversity impedes the team's performance when this congruence was not established. This is powerful, especially given that creating a sense of congruence took *as little as ten minutes* among team members, while the benefit for the team was experienced long into the future—an incredibly effective use of ten minutes. Take the time to start strong.

Communicate effectively

Language challenges happen in every global team as some members are often unequally fluent in their use of the lingua franca. Try these to avoid some of the greatest mistakes:

- Be both polite and clear in written and verbal communications. While polite speech might seem superfluous to direct communicators, there is less risk of something being misinterpreted as aggressive or rude.
- If you are the native language speaker, remember to speak slowly, rephrase frequently, and avoid culture-based slang.
- If you are a team member who is a nonnative speaker, ask your colleagues more frequently if your point is understood and ask them for clarification when needed. By initiating the questions as the nonnative speaker, your team members will have greater comfort in asking you to repeat or to clarify when needed.
- If you are the team leader, be mindful of how frequently you ask for spontaneous input because not all team members will be equally comfortable with brainstorming and on-the-spot idea generation due to language or culture. Instead, use agendas to allow team members to prepare.
- Be careful that the native speakers do not dominate the conversation and that all team members can share their thoughts. It also helps to rotate or designate someone to send summary notes after meetings.
- Meter the different communication styles for unintended consequences affecting the team functioning and call them out as objective differences and not ones to be misinterpreted. For example, when cross-cultural teams engage in a conversational flow, they will have positive feelings toward each other and have a heightened sense of belonging and connection to the group. Awkward silences break the conversational flow and, in doing so, make team members feel a sense of rejection and more negative feelings toward each other.[8] The definition of *awkward*, however,

differs across cultures. Silence starts to feel uncomfortable for English speakers after just four seconds, where as Japanese and Finnish speakers are comfortable with much longer periods of silence.

Foster relationships remotely

Your team will experience easier cultural integration when the team members genuinely like and care about each other. This can happen more naturally and is a bit easier when the team members are colocated. Given the challenges of the global pandemic and the ever-increasing use of geographically distributed teams, fostering connections needs to happen in virtual space. While it might feel contrived, I strongly recommend that each meeting begin with some form of rapport-building. For some cultures represented on your team, this might feel like a waste of time. However, when done successfully, the goodwill such rapport-building creates among team members is an important investment of time.

One of the easiest ways to foster relationships is to celebrate team members' personal and professional milestones, birthdays, and holidays. Whether to and how to celebrate these should be discussed as the team is forming to determine members' collective comfort with sharing these events. Some people are more private. That said, in most of the parts of the world where I have worked, having colleagues join each other in collective celebration is generally welcome if experienced from the position of sincere interest and respect and when no one person is made to feel uncomfortable.

Use collaborative technology mindfully

Collaborative technology is ubiquitous for global teams' collaboration. Many people assume that technology usage is culture-free. This is a myth. There are cross-cultural snags resulting from differences in how much information should be shared, how best to communicate, speed of communication, whether work (and technology) should interfere with personal time, and the like.

Technology can help facilitate your cultural integration if you can use it as a vehicle to increase trust before you use it to share information. There are different ways to accomplish this:

- Have regularly scheduled meetings (e.g., weekly, monthly, daily). The repetition of interaction increases liking and trust in many cultures.

- Rotate the start time to accommodate different time zones. Sharing the burden of time zone differences shows sensitivity to the inconvenience caused.
- When practical, try to answer emails, return calls, and provide materials in a timely fashion, during working hours. Faster responses increase trust, provided they are conveying an appropriate level of care for the request or communication.
- Use technology to include everyone in all team decisions (even more minor ones) unless the ground rules state otherwise. When everyone feels included, it is easier to foster team trust.
- Be respectful and do not schedule meetings on holidays which would be celebrated by some team members. In fact, respect and celebrate those holidays, if only with an appropriate greeting, whenever possible.
- Discuss the use of technology at the onset and use the lowest level of collaborative technology available to everyone on your team. It is a way to promote fairness and harmony.

Email, text, and other written communications

The written word does not eliminate culture differences. Consider this illustration: An employee writes a three-paragraph email to his or her manager with detailed rationale requesting additional resources for a project. The manager responds with a one-word email: "Approved." What this response positive or negative? Your perception is a function of your culture and your experiences. If you perceived the manager's response as positive, you likely believed that the employee probably provided a clear rationale for the request. If you perceived the manager's response as negative, you likely believed that the manager is rude, unhappy about the request, or does not really care about the project. The difference in these two perceptions is whether the email writer is from a low context culture (viewing the short response as supportive) or a high context culture (viewing the short response as negative or reluctant).

Video conferencing

To increase trust while on a video call, be sure to use cameras whenever possible and encourage others on the team to do the same. Another tip that helps tremendously in establishing trust on a video call is to look at the camera and not the screen, especially when you are speaking. For cultures that appreciate eye contact, it will seem as though you are making eye contact. In cultures where eye contact is less frequent, they will observe you as they would watch someone on television, and it will not feel uncomfortable because there would not be a perceived need to make eye contact in return.

Create a sense of community

To facilitate cultural integration, it is helpful for there to be a sense of community among the members of a culturally diverse group. Research has found that having a sense of community has four key features: membership, influence, integration and fulfillment of needs, and shared emotional connection.[9] When there is a sense of community, team members will identify with and feel committed to the team, feel as though they belong, and sense that they can rely on the other members of the team. When a sense of community is present, cultural integration forms deep roots because individuals within the community have a sense of commitment to each other and a greater sense of collective identity. They will defend the group's position over their own approach.

To help influence the creation of a sense of community to increase cultural integration, try some of these methods.

Foster membership

I am always surprised to learn the variance within a team on the extent to which team members *even realize* they are part of a team. Be certain to create the team's identity through its tangible purpose for being together. Also identify the team's uniqueness—highlighting the ways your team differs from all other teams.

Share influence

Be certain that all the members of the team have a voice in how the team will function. Everyone should each feel as though they matter in the way the team functions, how they collaborate, and the work they produce. If you observe a team member saying or doing something that could be perceived poorly by you or another on the team, ask for clarification on the behavior (and not your interpretation of the behavior). Allowing some team members to "steam roll over" other team members will damage psychological safety and the sense of influence each member should feel.

Fulfill needs

People want to feel as though they belong and have a shared sense of purpose. These are two basic psychological needs. To foster a greater sense of belonging, team members should be willing to help and support each other, irrespective of culture or location. A sense of purpose will be more deeply felt the more team members understand their goals, the importance of their goals, and the extent to which achievement of these goals affects the broader organization.

Create connection

To create connection within the team, encourage a spirit of gratitude and opportunities for shared happiness within the team. When team members feel appreciated by fellow team members, they have a heightened sense of belonging and commitment to the team. You can show gratitude to your fellow team members individually, authentically, and by highlighting their specific contributions. Just remember that public, personal recognition is appreciated in more individualistic cultures. Individual recognition could be embarrassing in collective cultures. To foster happiness within the team, you can celebrate group-level achievement and team milestones. This can also be achieved through shared memorable social activities, provided they are ones which would be equally appreciated among all team members.

How to build cultural integration

In addition to practicing the approaches from the previous sections, there are a variety of activities that will help you master cultural integration.

- Within your organization or functional area, identify policies or practices that were instituted globally. How was the acceptance (or resistance) to the practice felt around the world? What was done well? What could have been done differently?
- The most common use of cultural integration is in geographically distributed teams. Identify a few successful teams in your organization and speak with some team members about the strategies they used for communicating, sharing information, and building trust when forming the team. Try to identify what team formation practices worked well within your organization's culture.
- If you are currently part of a team, think of how your team's norms were formed. Did they evolve over time without discussion, were you socialized into them when you joined the team, or did you form them at the onset

when the team came together? How could having a team meeting on ground rules help the team's functioning?

- With any group you currently belong to, try to create a heightened sense of community. It is good to practice these skills with teams you understand well before trying the skills in a cross-cultural context. What worked? What did not?
- Speak with experts and bicultural colleagues about how teams will function differently across the two cultures they know well. Learning about the possible differences in team functioning can help you be more receptive to the cultural nuances of integration.

Key takeaways

- There are certain situations where culturally agile professionals need to engage in cultural integration, whereby they create a new set of norms representing no single cultural lens but integrating many.
- Professional activities needing an advanced level of cultural integration are mergers, acquisitions, joint ventures, global teams, creating new policies and practices, and conflict resolution.
- To effectively use cultural integration, you will need to first understand the range of perceptions and norms across the organizations, within the organization, within the team, or even between two people.
- If you are in a leadership role, help create psychological safety among your team members, so they feel safe to offer opinions and ideas, challenge each other, and take risks without personal or professional consequences.
- Be certain to learn about potential differences before you begin dialogue, use a positive tone about the benefit of differences, and focus on observable behaviors rather than subjective judgements.
- When in a global team, to foster greater cultural integration be sure to start strong, communicate effectively, build relationships remotely, use collaborative technology mindfully, and create community within the team.
- To help influence the creation of a sense of community to increase cultural integration, foster a sense of team membership, be certain there is an equally shared sense of influence, fulfill team members' needs for belonging and a sense of purpose, and create real connection of emotional bonds through expressions of gratitude and shared joy.

Keep reading

- Edmondson, A. C. 2018. *The Fearless Organization: Creating Psychological Safety in the Workplace for Learning, Innovation, and Growth*. Hoboken, NJ: Wiley.
- Gordon, J. 2018. *The Power of a Positive Team: Proven Principles and Practices That Make Great Teams Great*. Hoboken, NJ; Wiley.
- Hurt, K. 2020. *Courageous Cultures: How to Build Teams of Micro-Innovators, Problem Solvers, and Customer Advocates*. Nashville, TN: HarperCollins Leadership.
- McChrystal, S. 2015. *Team of Teams: New Rules of Engagement for a Complex World*. New York: Portfolio.
- Ryan, J. 2020. *Intangibles: Unlocking the Science and Soul of Team Chemistry*. New York: Little, Brown and Company.

Endnotes

1 Liu, C. Z. 2007. "Lenovo: An Example of Globalization of Chinese Enterprises." *Journal of International Business Studies* 384: 573–577.

2 Fernando, J. November 30, 2019. "A Look at Lenovo's Strategy and Business Model." Investopedia. https://www.investopedia.com/articles/investing/073015/look-lenovos-strategy-business-model.asp (archived at https://perma.cc/9TKP-ZXYG) [Accessed September 23, 2020].

3 Kraus, S. 1995. "Attitudes and the Prediction of Behavior: A Meta-Analysis of the Empirical Literature." *Personality and Social Psychology Bulletin* 21, no. 1: 58–75.

4 Erickson, T. February 6, 2009. "The Four Biggest Reasons for Generational Conflict in Teams." *Harvard Business Review*. hbr.org/2009/02/the-four-biggest-reasons-for-i (archived at https://perma.cc/WN64-L9V7) [Accessed September 10, 2020].

5 Swaab, R. I., Schaerer, M., Anicich, E. M., Ronay, R., and Galinsky, A. D. 2014. "The Too-Much-Talent Effect: Team Interdependence Determines When More Talent Is Too Much or Not Enough." *Psychological Science* 25, no. 8: 1581–1591.

6 Earley, P., and Mosakowski, E. 2000. "Creating Hybrid Team Cultures: An Empirical Test of Transnational Team Functioning." *Academy of Management Journal* 43, no. 1: 26–49.

7 Polzer, J. T., Milton, L. P., and Swarm, W. B. 2002. "Capitalizing on Diversity: Interpersonal Congruence in Small Work Groups." *Administrative Science Quarterly* 47, no. 2: 296–324.

8 Koudenburg, N., Postmes, T., and Gordijn, E. H. 2011. "Disrupting the Flow: How Brief Silences in Group Conversations Affect Social Needs." *Journal of Experimental Social Psychology* 47, no. 2: 512–515.

9 McMillan, D. W., and Chavis, D. M. 1986. "Sense of Community: A Definition and Theory." *Journal of Community Psychology* 14, no. 1: 6–23.

11 Using your cultural agility for career success

The cultural agility competencies in this book are critical for your success as you work with people from different cultures. These competencies will help you learn how to gain trust, build credibility, and communicate effectively. They will also help you make and execute the best decisions, even when the context is unfamiliar and unpredictable. Packaged together, these cultural agility competencies will propel your global, international, and multicultural career.

This final chapter includes my practical advice for your career success, including how to avoid cultural agility trip wires, develop from cross-cultural experiences, buffer yourself from culture shock, and find career fulfillment.

Avoid cultural agility trip wires

Cultural agility trip wires are blind spots created in unfamiliar cultures that make accurate observations more difficult. The three most troublesome cultural agility trip wires I have seen are those of *experience, technology*, and *similarity*. Aptly named, trip wires are practically invisible and work insidiously with the help of neuroscience to divert our attention. Unaware, we do a metaphorical cross-cultural face-plant. Even the most seasoned global professionals can miss cultural trip wires. However, if you are aware that they are out there, your focused attention will help you avoid them.

Trip wire 1: experience

When you ask someone about their cross-cultural experience, they often begin by sharing the number of countries in which they have worked or visited. They name *quantity* of cross-cultural experiences as an indicator of their cultural agility. This belief that a greater number of cross-cultural experiences makes a person culturally agile is one of the most prevalent trip wires I have observed.

At this point in the book, you know not to be impressed by passport stamps and frequent flyer miles because you understand that only deep cross-cultural experience will help you foster cultural agility. Breathing the air of another country is about as developmental for building cultural agility as Taco Tuesdays in the company cafeteria. While it is natural for people to think that their frequent travel equates to their cultural agility, most business and vacation travel provides only a superficial cross-cultural experience.

The more we travel for business or vacation, the more we are lulled into believing we are improving at working in other cultures. It is akin to playing the same miniature golf course for several years and believing that you are becoming an outstanding golfer. Overconfidence creates a blind spot that causes the *experience trip wire*. When faced with situations involving deeper cultural differences, people who have more superficial travel have no framework to understand the challenge—and are often surprised by the stumble.

Even longer-duration international experiences might need to be checked for these critical developmental properties. Sometimes longer experiences, such as international assignments and studying abroad, are spent surrounded by the cultural ease of compatriot communities, international clubs, international schools, and a corporate environment that feels much like home. A longer experience, however, has greater potential for a deeper developmental experience.

Trip wire 2: technology

There is a broad assumption that the more we use collaborative technology, the less need there is to worry about cultural differences. On the contrary, this *technology trip wire* is problematic because people underestimate the cultural differences associated with information sharing, text and chat communications, asynchronous collaboration, and even preferences for technology usage. Our cultural norms will influence how we use email, video calls, and texting. It is easy to miss the effect of culture because of the ease and speed of communicating.

Think about what it would take to travel to another country for a meeting—a passport, plane ticket, hotel, and so on. The effort alone is a reminder that you are in a different place. Compare that effort with the ease with which you can click on a link for a conference call. The same meeting required about thirty seconds of preparation, without any effortful reminder of being "in" a different culture. Just remember that technology, while convenient, does not subdue the importance of cultural differences.

Trip wire 3: similarity

The cosmopolitan culture of today has homogenized the perceptual cues of well-educated professionals and university students. Among this higher socioeconomic status group, there is worldwide similarity around their manner of dress, music enjoyed, luxury items coveted, ethnic restaurants frequented, and so on. This *similarity trip wire* stems from the omission of visual cues to trigger the expectation that someone might be ascribing to a different set of cultural norms and values. Without the visual prompt, we assume more similarity and fewer cultural differences.

The use of English around the world has made this similarity trip wire a bit more difficult to see. According to the statistics compiled by Lemon Grad, there are almost 400 million native English speakers.[1] However, nearly twice that number speak English as a second language, almost all of them in the ranks of the well-educated and professional people worldwide. Over 50 percent of internet content and information in scientific journals is in English. When we can communicate with ease with other professionals, we again can forget that deeper cultural differences remain.

Develop from cross-cultural experiences

Some things are timeless, such as the following words of René Descartes from nearly 400 years ago, describing how developmental cross-cultural experiences can be.[2]

> It is good to know something of the customs of various peoples, so as to judge our own more soundly and so as not to think that everything that is contrary to our ways is ridiculous and against reason, as those who have seen nothing have

a habit of doing. But when one takes too much time traveling, one eventually becomes a stranger in one's own culture.

Spending time in different countries and with people from other cultures has the potential to be highly developmental; however, as noted earlier, merely breathing the air of another country will not build cultural agility. Trust me, if I could build everyone's cultural agility through international travel, I would have started a fund to ensure every human could take a cruise in another part of the world, without any need to get off the ship. Voilà, world peace. Ludicrous, of course. It is just not that easy.

For a cultural experience to be developmental, you need to experience contextual novelty—to have the feeling of your expectations not matching reality and, therefore, not quite knowing how to interpret behaviors (or, if you think you do, getting it wrong). Developmental cross-cultural experiences will widen your brain's store of interpretations while questioning the assumptions you make about the context.

Unless certain features of a cross-cultural experience are present, time spent working or visiting other cultures keeps us on the periphery of those cultures. My colleagues and I conducted a series of studies and found that for an experience to be developmental, it needs to have three of the following features.[3]

Having high-quality interactions

High-quality interactions with peers from different countries and cultures are fundamental for development because they enable the dialogue which will help us understand the contextual differences. The more time peers have together and the more they are required to collaborate, the greater their challenges. Peer-level colleagues from different cultures who are collaborating for three months will likely have more potential for meaningful interactions than the same two colleagues attending a three-day corporate retreat.

These high-quality interactions are fundamental to your ability to continually develop cultural agility. Never miss an opportunity to form a collaborative relationship with a peer from another culture. Use your relationship management competencies to continue to build cultural agility through your interactions with others.

Understanding the limits of skills and abilities in a different cultural context

A truly developmental experience will enable us to question our assumptions about how things are done and test the limits of our knowledge in the new context. These experiences will allow us to use our skills and abilities in situations where we need to fully understand the context before we can be successful. As you have more of these experiences, you begin to build a repertoire for what will work—and where. Over time, these experiences build your cultural agility by improving your ability to understand the knowledge, skills, and abilities in a different cultural context and to reproduce culturally appropriate skills and behaviors when appropriate.[4]

Placing yourself in situations where you will need to test your skills and abilities in a different cultural context is not always the most comfortable way to work, but it is one of the most valuable ways to build cultural agility. You can rely on your self-management competencies to propel your ability to develop cultural agility as you push the limits of your contextual understanding.

Receiving feedback on effectiveness

For cultural experiences to be truly developmental, they should include opportunities for receiving feedback on whether you are behaving in a way that aligns with your intended perception. Receiving feedback from peers, cultural coaches, and leaders is one way for this to occur. Another way is to seek it by asking if there is some way you could be better received as being credible, trustworthy, and engaged, etc. Ideally, these experiences should happen at times when making cultural or linguistic mistakes would not be embarrassing or professionally risky.

It is difficult for many people to ask for (and receive) feedback. Allow yourself to be coachable just as you would be if you were learning any other new skill. Just as a coach helps you build skills, learning to interpret and succeed in a new cultural context requires the help of someone with insider knowledge. Instead of expecting that you will not make cultural mistakes, change your frame of reference to the assumption that you will make mistakes without the help of others. You can rely on your competencies of humility, resilience, and tolerance of ambiguity to help you build your cultural agility even further.

Buffer from culture shock

If you will be spending a longer period in a high-quality cross-cultural experience, your cultural agility will help you succeed and will also help you adjust to the new culture. Especially when working in another country, your cultural agility acts as an emotional safety harness for the roller coaster of emotions you will likely experience. Many researchers have noted the predictable highs and lows, otherwise known as the adjustment curve, associated with living in another country. Some phases of the adjustment curve are pleasurable or emotionally neutral, while others are more difficult. With a higher level of cultural agility, you will be able to handle the emotional challenges of the more difficult phases with relative ease.

For everyone, adjusting to living in another country will take time, but the speed to adjustment will also depend on your level of cultural agility. Thus, our goal is to minimize the length of time spent in the difficult phases and maximize the speed of adjustment. To better recognize the importance of cultural agility to help move through the adjustment curve, consider the following phases.

Anticipatory adjustment

In the anticipatory adjustment phase, you are still in your familiar surroundings (e.g., at home if relocating, with a current employer if changing companies). At this point, you might have agreed to accept an international assignment, decided to attend school in another country, or accepted a new job. Once you have decided to make the move, you might be filled with excitement and happiness but possibly also thinking about the things you will miss. You might experience some negative emotions anticipating what it will be like to be away from trusted colleagues, family, and friends.

Honeymoon

In the honeymoon phase, often associated with relocating to another country, you have just arrived in the host country and have spent the first days, weeks, and maybe even months enjoying the new and novel experiences that surround you. During the honeymoon phase, you have heightened sensory awareness. It is natural to have a sense of mindfulness when the sights, sounds, smells, and tastes are all new and different. You are experiencing the host country's culture with greater awe and, in this phase, you will likely feel overly optimistic and happy about the opportunity to live abroad. You might experience a honeymoon phase when you start a new job, relocate to a new neighborhood, and so on.

Cultural shock

Just as in marriage, the honeymoon will eventually wear off and the less flattering reality of the host country or new company will become more salient. In this cultural shock phase, the steepest downward emotional slope, many people experience some frustration, stress, and anxiety about living in their host country and new neighborhood or working for a new employer. Especially in the context of living in a host country, these feelings are often associated with the sense that one does not necessarily fit in, does not really belong, cannot communicate well, and is ineffective. In this phase, many people begin to compare an idealized view of what they had before (previous employer, home country) to everything they perceive as inferior in the new context. In this phase, people often seek out the company of compatriots or other people who are considered outsiders. The culture shock phase can last a few days or can be experienced over many months.

Adjustment

Eventually, the emotional roller coaster begins to be less of a dramatic ride. In this adjustment phase, you see the host country or new employer realistically, for both its positive and negative features. Your social circle, trusted group of colleagues, and support network deepen, as you create your sense of belonging. At this point, you might have adjusted your expectations for communication and professional effectiveness and are feeling positive about your ability to succeed in the host country. In this phase, you feel much like you felt before the change or relocation—with both good days and bad days.

Anticipatory departure

If you are working or studying in another country, unless you plan to remain there, you will likely be ready to complete your international assignment, graduate from the university, or accept a role in another location. In other words, you are winding down your time in the current situation and are beginning to anticipate your departure or next move. International assignees and study abroad students can experience anxiety at the thought of leaving their host country because they sense that they did not do all the things they had hoped to do during their stint abroad. It is natural to believe there was always more to see and do.

Repatriation

If you have lived abroad, there is often a repatriation phase of returning to the place you called home, where you can reengage with friends, family members, and things you enjoy doing. At first, you will enjoy a reverse honeymoon phase at home. As you are reconnecting with loved ones, enjoying your favorite foods, and engaging in your favorite activities, you will likely be viewing them in the most positive light and with full mindfulness. You are on another honeymoon, after all. If friends and family are interested in hearing about your experiences in the host country, you might even feel special and admired for having accomplished something unique. Over time, the second honeymoon ends, and you adjust to being back home. As before, some days are better than other; the dramatic ride is over, at least until your next big move.

It is important to note that during this repatriation phase, people who have developed the greatest level of cultural agility often find themselves feeling unsettled, unfulfilled, or bored when they are surrounded by the familiarity of home. It might be the case that they no longer feel unique or special, maybe as people stop asking about their experiences abroad. It might be that they sense that they no longer fit in at home as well as they once did. Their identity might have changed as they feel more cosmopolitan or global. If that is the case, they often seek their next culturally novel experience for ongoing career fulfillment.

Building cultural agility to find career fulfillment is the final section of this book.

Find career fulfillment

Some people who have a positive first experience traveling abroad will describe themselves as being bitten by the travel bug. They want to continue to explore the many interesting places in the world. If they are hardwired to continually seek novelty, they are likely to study abroad when in school, take vacations off the beaten path, and seek out international assignments when they start their professional careers. As culturally agile people, they appreciate and value cultural diversity both personally and professionally. They tend to have a diverse group of friends, live in more diverse neighborhoods, and marry people from other cultures. In the professional context, they are magnetically drawn to culturally diverse experiences throughout their careers.

Researcher Vesa Suutari and his colleagues describe this magnetic draw as an international career orientation or career anchor.[5] As originally discovered by researcher Edgar Schein, career anchors are motivating factors that propel people to make career decisions consistent with their self-identities and values.[6] In addition to an international career anchor, he identified the other career anchors, such as autonomy, security, creativity, and work-life balance. Based on Schein's career anchors, which do you most want from your career?

- Are you motivated for a career in which you can be a technical expert? Would you like to be so good at what you do professionally that your expert advice will be sought out and appreciated?
- Are you motivated for a career in which you will lead people? Would you like to oversee a business unit, making decisions that affect many people and directing the work of others?
- Are you motivated for a career in which you can exercise autonomy and have full independence? Would you like to have the freedom to do a job your own way and on your own schedule?
- Are you motivated for a career which provides security and stability? Would you like stable employment and financial security?
- Are you motivated for a career in which you can be entrepreneurial? Would you like to start and run your own business?
- Are you motivated for a career in which you can be creative and innovative? Would you like to have a career in the arts, design, innovation, and the like?
- Are you motivated for a career in which you can work for the greater good of society or be dedicated to a higher purpose? Do you want to always feel as though you are serving others in the sense of a shared humanity? Would you like to contribute and use your talents in the service of others?
- Are you motivated for a career in which you can be competitive and challenged? Would you like a career in which you can solve problems or compete in situations where few can excel or win?

- Are you motivated for a career in which you can enjoy a healthy work/life balance? Would you like a career that will permit you to harmonize all important aspects of your life (e.g., your personal life, family, career)?
- Are you motivated for a career in which you will work internationally, in different countries and with people from different cultures? Would you like a career that enables you to travel and experience novel environments and diversity?

For all anchors, according to Schein's seminal work, when a career choice is presented, the anchor will guide the choice such that each successive career move is self-reinforcing. The anchor becomes heavier, so to speak. For culturally agile professionals with an international career anchor, they cannot imagine any other type of career. Their careers would not be fulfilling without the opportunity to work in different countries and with people from different cultures.

Motivation for a cross-cultural career

Researchers Mila Lazarova, Jean-Luc Cerdin, and Yuan Liao developed a scale to assess the international career anchor.[7] Do any of the following items, based on their research, apply to you? Make an X next to each item for which you would respond "yes." Try not to overthink any question. Usually your first answer is your best one.

- ☐ Would you turn down or leave a job if you did not have the opportunity to work internationally?
- ☐ Are you attracted to the idea of working in another country?
- ☐ Is your sense of success determined by the extent to which you have an international career?
- ☐ Do you envision your perfect career to be an international one?
- ☐ Do you want your career to include international travel?

This self-assessment is merely a way to provide you with some insights about the strength of your international career anchor. If you checked off all of these, you likely have a heavy international career anchor. For you, gaining cultural agility will hold a deeper sense of meaning as it will be core to your self-evaluation, identity, and ultimate career fulfillment.

What if you *do not* have an international career anchor? If your career has you working in different countries and with people from different cultures, cultural agility remains a critical competency for your professional success in a multicultural work setting. In fact, Suutari and his colleagues determined that only half of all professionals who had accepted international assignments had an international career anchor. The others had a different anchor, and they were reflected in the other reasons to accept an international assignment: They either wanted the income boost associated with the assignment, wanted to be responsive to a supervisor who made the request, or felt a sense of obligation to the company or the project. While everyone with an international career needs cultural agility, not everyone has an international career anchor.

Whether working in different countries or with people from different cultures is an internal passion or a necessary competency to advance your career, I hope this book has provided a springboard for development.

Build your cultural agility

As a reader of *Build Your Cultural Agility*, you might be interested in MyGiide, an app to help build your cultural agility. You can access MyGiide for free assessments of your cross-cultural values and cultural agility competencies. Through MyGiide, you can also purchase cultural coaching sessions, action plans for development, culture-specific information, and access to webinars.

Scan the QR code to access MyGiide (www.mygiide.com).

Stay connected

I would welcome the opportunity to stay connected with you. Please follow me on LinkedIn for additional posts and insights about cultural agility:

https://www.linkedin.com/in/paulacaligiuri/ (archived at https://perma.cc/K2BK-MCEJ).

Endnotes

1 Liu, C. Z. 2007. "Lenovo: An Example of Globalization of Chinese Enterprises." *Journal of International Business Studies* 384: 573–577.

2 Fernando, J. November 30, 2019. "A Look at Lenovo's Strategy and Business Model." Investopedia. https://www.investopedia.com/articles/investing/073015/look-lenovos-strategy-business-model.asp (archived at https://perma.cc/9TKP-ZXYG) [Accessed September 23, 2020].

3 Kraus, S. 1995. "Attitudes and the Prediction of Behavior: A Meta-Analysis of the Empirical Literature." *Personality and Social Psychology Bulletin* 21, no. 1: 58–75.

4 Erickson, T. February 6, 2009. "The Four Biggest Reasons for Generational Conflict in Teams." *Harvard Business Review*. hbr.org/2009/02/the-four-biggest-reasons-for-i (archived at https://perma.cc/WN64-L9V7) [Accessed September 10, 2020].

5 Swaab, R. I., Schaerer, M., Anicich, E. M., Ronay, R., and Galinsky, A. D. 2014. "The Too-Much-Talent Effect: Team Interdependence Determines When More Talent Is Too Much or Not Enough." *Psychological Science* 25, no. 8: 1581–1591.

6 Earley, P., and Mosakowski, E. 2000. "Creating Hybrid Team Cultures: An Empirical Test of Transnational Team Functioning." *Academy of Management Journal* 43, no. 1: 26–49.

7 Polzer, J. T., Milton, L. P., and Swarm, W. B. 2002. "Capitalizing on Diversity: Interpersonal Congruence in Small Work Groups." *Administrative Science Quarterly* 47, no. 2: 296–324.

8 Koudenburg, N., Postmes, T., and Gordijn, E. H. 2011. "Disrupting the Flow: How Brief Silences in Group Conversations Affect Social Needs." *Journal of Experimental Social Psychology* 47, no. 2: 512–515.

9 McMillan, D. W., and Chavis, D. M. 1986. "Sense of Community: A Definition and Theory." *Journal of Community Psychology* 14, no. 1: 6–23.

Index

accents 109
accuracy 34, 66, 117–20, 121
acquisitions 169
action-oriented coping strategies 68, 69–70
active listening 102, 105, 118, 119
active responding 102
adjustment curve 187–89
adjustment phase 188
adventure seeking traits 25, 32
Afghanistan 59, 130–32
agendas 12, 174
Air, Euan 93–96
alternative explanations 124
alternative opinions 125
ambiguity tolerance 22, 23–41
ambiguity tolerance self-assessment 27–28
anticipatory adjustment phase 187
anticipatory departure phase 188–89
anxiety 36, 67–68, 99, 104, 105, 188, 189
appreciation 89
  see also gratitude
Argentina 155
assignments, international 38, 68, 183, 187–89
assistance, asking for 88
assumptions 26, 81, 126
Australia 4, 103, 140
authenticity 80, 89, 118, 144–45, 156, 173
authority 8–9, 140, 157, 158, 159
autism spectrum disorders 116
autonomy 141, 160, 162, 164, 190
awkward silences 174–75

balance-motivated cultures 14
barriers, communication 103, 110
behavior focus 171–72
behavior motivation 55, 160–62
behavioral training 156
belonging 105, 108, 160, 161, 162, 174, 177–78, 188
bicultural colleagues 56, 71, 179
bilingual individuals 118
black-and-white thinking 30, 33–34
blaming others 66
Born, Dr Dana 58–61
boundary violation 144, 146–47
bowing 107
brain science 2, 3, 6–7, 28–30, 101, 121–22, 148
Brandt, Martin 36, 38–39
Brazil 108
broaden-and-build approach 66, 78
buddy programs 53–54, 71

Canada 123, 140
Careem 93, 94
career fulfillment 189–92
career orientation (anchor) 190–92
caste (class-bound society) 13
categorization 28–29
celebrations 175, 178
cell (mobile) phones 79, 103
challenge sharing 149
challenges, learning from 55–56
Chastain, Christine 112–15
childhood 47
China 106, 107, 123, 141
closing eyes 119
coaching 44, 69, 71, 89, 109, 149, 150, 161, 169, 186
coconut cultures 108
cognitive dissonance 136–37
cognitive processing 121–22, 149
collaboration 24, 79, 171, 175–76, 185
  peer-level 38, 109, 185
collaborative technology 175–76
collectivist (group) cultures 9, 123–24, 157, 158, 160, 162, 163, 178
commitment 159, 161, 178
communication 102–03, 155, 170, 174–75
  barriers to 110
  direct (low-context) 11–12, 83–84, 123, 161, 174, 176
  written 11, 176
  see also conversations; feedback; language skills; listening skills
community-building 177–78, 179
competition 84
conceptual level perspective taking 115–16
confidence building 52–54, 144

confirmation bias 118
conflict resolution 168, 173
connectedness 118, 160, 161, 162, 178
consistency 44, 132, 145, 153, 159, 163–64
consultants 123
context 87, 89, 90, 133, 186
contextual novelty 5, 6, 7, 35–36, 37, 185
control 13, 72
controlled-time cultures 12–13
conversational flow 108, 174–75
conversations 37, 104–05, 107–08
coping strategies 68–70, 72–73
corporate values 154, 156, 164
corporate volunteer programs 36, 37, 38–39
Covid-19 96, 147–49
creatives 115
creativity 50–51, 78, 79, 113, 115, 124, 130, 139
cross-cultural training 16, 101, 142, 170
cultural adaptation 133, 135–52, 167, 170
cultural agility, defined 15, 17
cultural agility self-assessment 2
cultural context 87, 89, 90, 133, 186
cultural differences, defined 3–4
cultural insiders 26, 123, 150, 154, 186
cultural integration 133, 167–81
cultural metaphors 6
cultural minimization 130, 133, 153–66, 167, 169–70
cultural outsiders 21, 26, 154, 188
cultural shock phase 188
culture, defined 3
curiosity 22, 42–57
curiosity self-assessment 46

decision-making speed 29–30, 34–35
defensiveness 50, 170, 171
demographic similarity 29, 102, 120, 125
Denmark 123
desired outcomes 149, 154
D4 32, 67
direct (low-context) communication cultures 11–12, 83–84, 123, 161, 174, 176
diversity 104, 156, 173–74, 190
dopamine 15, 32, 47, 67
DRD4 32

early-life curiosity 47
egalitarian cultures 8–9, 119, 123, 140, 157, 162
eight dimensions of culture framework 7–14
emails 11, 34, 119, 173, 176
emotion-focused coping strategies 69, 70, 72–73
emotional level perspective taking 115–16
emotions, negative 61, 66
empaths 116
empathy 66–67, 79, 107, 112–27
English language usage 184
ethnocentricity 82–83
exercise 70, 73
expectation vs experience mismatch 2–3
experience 31, 35–39, 46, 97, 120–21, 183
see also international assignments; international volunteering
experiential similarity 120–21
expression of humility 83–84
expression of perspective taking 122–24
external control 13
extraversion 99–100
see also openness
eye contact 103, 176–77
see also closing eyes

Facebook 93, 96
facilitation 114, 169
familiarity 31, 37, 105
feedback 11, 24, 80, 82, 86–87, 89–90, 143, 150, 161, 186
feminism 114–15
fight-or-flight mechanism 28–29
Finland 143–44, 175
firing employees 157
first impressions 35, 145
5-HTTLPR gene 67–68
fixed mindset 88
flexible boundaries 146–47
fluid-time cultures 12–13
formal cultures 7–8, 119
France 107, 155
frequency of interactions 100–01, 105
friendship bonds 104–05

generational culture 1, 172
genetics 15, 24–25, 32–33, 67–68
Germany 4, 108, 123
gestures 11, 119, 121, 139
GlaxoSmithKline (GSK) 38, 43, 44
global teams 38, 172–78
global virtual teams 168
Global Zero Work Site Hazard Project 162–63
goal setting 138, 145, 150
graduate entrants 17, 85, 104
gratitude 71, 89, 130, 178, 179
Greece 107
Greetings 107, 110, 139, 144, 148, 149, 176

ground rules 169, 172, 173, 176
group (collectivist) cultures 9, 123–24, 157, 158, 160, 162, 163, 178
growth mindset 53, 66–67, 72–73, 78, 81, 86, 87–88
GSK (GlaxoSmithKline) 38, 43, 44

handshakes 10, 107, 131, 132, 148
head tilting 103, 110
hierarchical cultures 8, 123, 140, 157, 162
high contact cultural experience 36, 37
high-context (indirect) communication cultures 11–12, 83–84, 123, 161, 176
high-quality interactions 185
Hijo Resources Corporation 44–45
holidays 175, 176
honeymoon phase 187–88
host national colleagues 38, 53–54, 58–59, 69, 70, 95, 100, 109, 130
hubris 84, 85
humility 75, 77–92
humility self-assessment 81–82
hybrid approaches 145, 168, 173
hybrid teams 168, 173
hygiene perspective 38, 132

IBM 169
inauthenticity 144–45
see also authenticity
incompetence, feelings of 144, 150
India 24, 109, 113–15, 123
indirect (high-context) communication cultures 11–12, 83–84, 123, 161, 176
individualistic cultures 9–10, 141, 157, 160, 178
Indonesia 23, 24, 139, 163
influence 115, 138, 158, 164, 165, 177, 179
see also persuasion
influence sharing 177
informal cultures 8
initial interest 51–52
insiders 26, 123, 150, 154, 186
interactions 97, 100–01, 105, 185
interdependent teams 172–78
intermediaries 123
internal control 13
international assignments 38, 68, 183, 187–89
international career orientation (anchor) 190–92
international career orientation (anchor) self-assessment 191–92
international students 36–37, 103–05, 141
international volunteering 36, 37, 38–39
interpersonal understanding 10, 49, 51, 93–111
interpretation, perceptual differences 121–22
interruption 107–08
introversion 100
Iran 93, 107
Italy 52, 107

Japan 4, 107, 119, 139, 146, 175
job titles 140–41
joint ventures 169
Jordan 94
judgements 6, 30, 34–35, 171–72, 179
Jung, Kimberley 129–33
junior staff 90

Kalashnikov Index 96
Kenya 38–39
kissing 107, 148
knowledge 25, 48–49, 78–80, 81, 95
Korea 107

language skills 38, 48, 72, 85, 95, 174–75, 184
laws 114, 138
'lazy brain' problem 3, 7
leadership 83, 100, 138, 140, 156, 158, 169
leaning forward 103
Lenovo 169
lessons learned interviews 164
liking 31, 105, 146, 158, 159, 175
'limited seating' training programs 160
listening skills 44, 55, 102, 105, 118, 119
local knowledge 25, 78–80, 95
'lone star' team member 172–73
longer-duration international assignments 183
loose national cultures 4
low contact cultural experience 36, 37
low-context (direct) communication cultures 11–12, 83–84, 123, 161, 174, 176

Major League Baseball 173
mastery 160, 161, 164, 165
MBA graduates 85
meaning (purpose) 14, 160, 161, 177–78
meditation 32, 33, 72, 73, 86
meetings 69, 174, 175–76
mental resistance 142, 144–47, 150
mergers 44, 169, 170, 179
messenger choice 155
Middle East 93–94, 96, 124, 140

milestone celebrations 175, 178
mindfulness 33, 40, 72, 187, 189
minute markers 35
mirroring 95, 103, 110, 146
mistakes 22, 58–59, 62, 88, 89, 90, 186
mobile phones 79, 103
modeling behaviors 79, 84, 89, 144, 150, 157–58
moderate contact cultural experience 37
motivation 55, 160–62
multigenerational teams 172
MyGiide 3, 7, 192

national culture 1, 4
National Football League 173
National Military Academy of Afghanistan 59
native language speakers 174
need for cognition 46, 48, 50
negative emotions 61, 66
negative self-talk 53
Nepal 77, 79
Netherlands 83, 107
networks 58–59, 69, 93–111, 154, 170
  support 70–71, 82, 87, 113–14, 188
  see also bicultural colleagues; host national colleagues
new cultural norms 149, 167–81
Nigeria 77, 80, 95
9/11 attacks 59–60
nonanswers 147
nonnative speakers 174
nonnormative behavior, expressing 149
norms 5–7, 49, 148, 155–57, 164
  new 149, 167–81
  social 4, 8, 123, 148, 159, 165
  team 178–79
novelty seeking 15, 49

observation 56, 142, 143
offending, fear of 146
older generation work habits 172
openness 32, 37, 99–100, 109, 120
  see also extraversion
optimism 59, 61, 65, 68, 72, 73, 129
organizational culture 1
outcome focus 72, 149, 154
outsiders 21, 26, 154, 188
overconfidence 183

pattern recognition 11, 49, 56, 99
peach cultures 108
peer-level collaboration 38, 109, 185
perception, control over 147
perceptual level perspective taking 115–16
personal boundaries 144, 146–47
personality 15, 32–33, 67–68, 99–100
perspective taking 72, 73, 76, 112–27
perspective taking self-assessment 116–17
persuasion 154, 158–60, 163, 164, 165
  see also influence
Philippines 23, 25, 42, 44
physical health 72
policy 113–15, 138, 168, 178
positive affect 66, 71
positive regard 147
positivity 170–71
posture 95, 103, 119
power 162
practice 16, 33–35, 149, 163–64
praising others 89, 157, 160
preferred state selling situations 139–40
privacy 122, 123
private equity sector 139–40
problem-focused coping strategies 68, 69–70
productivity 141
professional networks 1, 93–111
professional sports teams 172–73
proximity of interactions 100–01
purpose (meaning) 14, 160, 161, 177–78

questioning skills
  relationship-management 80, 88–90, 102, 105, 122, 126
  self-management 23, 43–44, 47, 50, 54
  task-management 138, 143–44, 174

rapport-building 175
reciprocation 130, 158, 165
recognition 9, 157, 178
recruitment 156–57
reflection 73, 86
reframing 71–72, 94, 144–45
regional culture 1
regular interactions 100–01
regulations 13, 18, 138, 149, 165
relationship building 51, 52, 75–76, 93–111, 171
relationship building self-assessment 98–99
relationship management competencies 75–128, 175
relationship-oriented cultures 106, 123, 141, 162
remote relationships 175
repatriation 189
research 54–55, 69
resentment, overcoming 145–46
resilience, defined 61–62
resilience competencies 22, 53, 58–74
resilience self-assessment 63–64

respect 23, 39, 43–44, 80, 81, 119, 121, 132, 137, 176
response techniques 102
retail sector 139
revising views 81
rewards 157, 160, 162
rigid boundaries 146–47
Robinson, Graham 162–63
Rumi Spice 131–32, 133, 153
Russia 108
Rwanda 77–78

safety standards 93–94, 155, 162–63
scarcity 159–60
scarification 80
security standards 93–94
Segismundo, Ramon 42–45
self-assessments 2, 27–28, 46, 63–64, 98–99, 116–17, 191–92
self-awareness 34, 63, 81, 86–87, 98, 116
self-centeredness 84
self-disclosure 8, 102, 105, 108, 122–23
self-efficacy 65, 73, 160, 161
self-interest (individualistic) cultures 9–10, 141, 157, 160, 178
self-management competencies 21–74
self-reflection 73, 86
selling situations 138, 139–40
serotonin 67–68
shared interests 101–02, 120
shared meaning 156
shared values 156
Shaye, Dr David 77–80
Shell 162–63
silence 107–08, 174–75
similarities 101–02, 104–05, 120–21, 125, 173, 184
similarity effect exercise 125
small steps 72
smiling 30, 102–03, 107
smoking policies 113–15
sociability 100
social activities 105, 178
social connections 118
social distance 96, 107, 110, 148
social learning 143–44, 150, 170
social media 49, 84
see also Facebook
social norms 4, 8, 123, 148, 159, 164, 165
socialization 154–58
socialized extraverts 100
socializing agents 124–25
Somoano, Cheryl 23–26
Spain 107
sports activities 70, 109, 120, 172–73
sports teams 109, 172–73
standards 94, 132, 133, 138, 149, 153–54, 164, 167, 168
status-oriented cultures 14
stereotyping 4, 26–27, 29, 31
stress management techniques 71–72
stress responses 21, 26, 62–63, 66
stretch experiences 36–39, 64–67
structured conversations 37
students 36–37, 52, 103–05, 141
subjective judgements 6, 172
subjective norms 155–56, 164
successful experiences 53
summary notes 174
support networks 58, 70–71, 82, 87, 97, 105, 113–14, 188
surgical scouts 79
Sweden 123
symptom-focused (emotion-focused) coping strategies 69, 70, 72–73

target cultures 48, 55, 56, 90
task-management competencies 129–81
task-oriented cultures 123, 162
team agendas 12, 174
team charters 173
team congruence 173–74
team formation 178
team leaders 79, 174
team norms 178–79
teams 12, 38, 79, 109, 168, 172–79
technology 175–76, 183–84
Thailand 84, 139, 146
tight national cultures 4
tone of voice 84, 119, 143
touching 107, 148
training 16, 94, 101, 142, 156, 160, 170
transactional cultures 10–11
trip wires 182–84
trust 95–96, 101, 123, 130–31, 132, 138, 139–40, 170–71, 173

United Arab Emirates (UAE) 93, 94
United Kingdom 103, 141
United States (US) 43, 78, 103, 107, 108, 113–14, 123, 155, 157, 173
unspoken assumptions 26

value judgements 171–72
values 5–7, 49, 154, 156–57, 164
video-conferencing 176–77
virtual teams 168
visual cues 119, 184
visual level perspective taking 115–16
volunteering 36, 37, 38–39, 129

Ward, Steve 169
'When in Rome' analogy 135–37
work outcomes 140–41
written communication 11, 176

Yang, Yuanqing 169
younger generation work habits 172

Zimbabwe 77, 79

Printed in the USA
CPSIA information can be obtained
at www.ICGtesting.com
JSHW041321201223
54094JS00018B/250

9 781789 666595